Small
HOME PLANS

GARLINGHOUSE

Library of Congress No: 92-075093

ISBN: 0-938708-45-7

Submit all Canadian plan orders to:

The Garlinghouse Company
20 Cedar Street North
Kitchener, Ontario N2H 2WB
Canadians Orders only: 1-800-561-4169
Fax #: 1-519-743-1282
Customer Service #: 1-519-743-4169

TABLE OF CONTENTS

Photography by Charles Brooks Photography

No. 34029

*S*kylight Brightens Master Bedroom

Keep dry during the rainy season under the
covered porch entryway of this gorgeous home.
A foyer separates the dining room, with a
decorative ceiling, from the breakfast area and
kitchen. Off the kitchen, conveniently located, is
the laundry room. The living room features a
vaulted beamed ceiling and fireplace. Located
between the living room and two bedrooms, both
with large closets, is a full bath. On the other side
of the living room is the master bedroom. The
master bedroom not only has a decorative ceiling,
but also a skylight above the entrance of its
private bath. The double-vanitied bathroom
features a large walk-in closet. For those who
enjoy outdoor living, an optional deck is offered,
accessible through sliding glass doors off of this
wonderful master bedroom. Please indicate slab,
crawlspace or basement foudation when ordering.

Main living area — 1,686 sq. ft.
Garage — 491 sq. ft.

Total living area — 1,686 sq. ft.

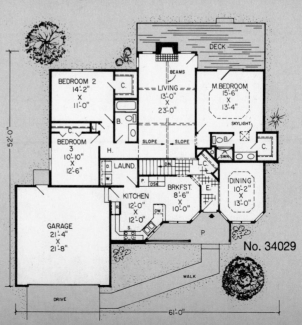

No. 34029

*M*aster Retreat Crowns Spacious Home

Here's a compact beauty with a wide-open feeling. Step past the inviting front porch, and savor a breathtaking view of active areas: the columned entry with its open staircase and windows high overhead; the soaring living room, divided from the kitchen and dining room by the towering fireplace chimney; and the screened porch beyond the triple living room windows. Tucked behind the stairs, you'll find a cozy parlor. And, across the hall, a bedroom with an adjoining full bath features access to the screened porch. Upstairs, the master suite is an elegant retreat you'll want to come home for, with its romantic dormer window seat, private balcony, and double-vanitied bath.

First floor — 1,290 sq. ft.
Second floor — 405 sq. ft.
Screened porch — 152 sq. ft.
Garage — 513 sq. ft.

Total living area — 1,695 sq. ft.

No. 19422

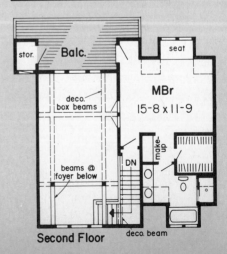

stor. | Balc. | seat

deco. box beams

MBr
15-8 x 11-9

beams @ foyer below

DN | make-up

Second Floor | deco. beam

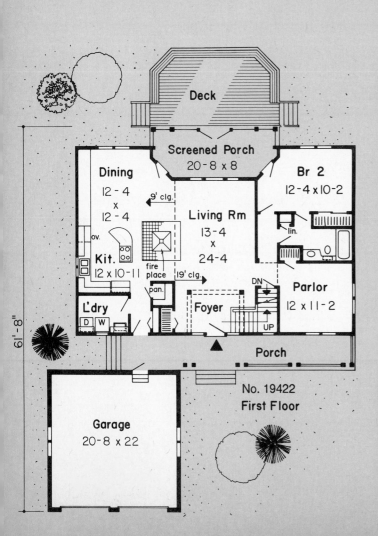

Deck

Screened Porch
20 - 8 x 8

Dining
12 - 4
x
12 - 4

9' clg.

Br 2
12-4 x10-2

Living Rm
13 - 4
x
24 - 4

lin.

ov.

Kit.
12 x 10-11

fire
place

19' clg.

DN

Parlor
12 x 11-2

L'dry
D W

pan.

Foyer

UP

Porch

No. 19422
First Floor

Garage
20-8 x 22

6'-1" - 8"

High Impact in a Small Package

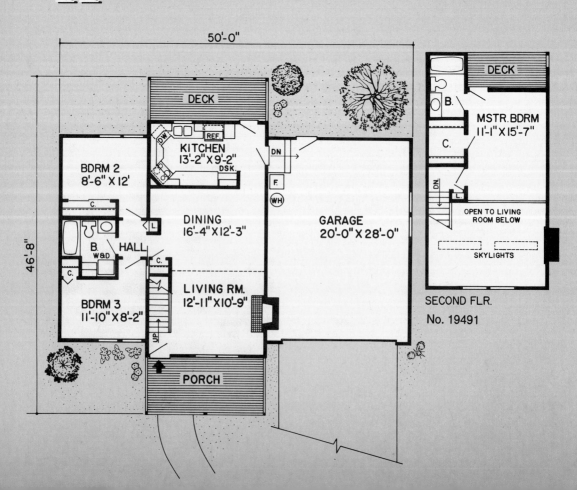

50'-0"

46'-8"

DECK

KITCHEN
13'-2" X 9'-2"

REF.

DW.

DSK.

DN

F.

WH

BDRM 2
8'-6" X 12'

C.

L

DINING
16'-4" X 12'-3"

GARAGE
20'-0" X 28'-0"

B.
W&D

HALL

C.

LIVING RM.
12'-11" X 10'-9"

BDRM 3
11'-10" X 8'-2"

UP

PORCH

DECK

B.

MSTR. BDRM
11'-1" X 15'-7"

C.

DN

L

OPEN TO LIVING
ROOM BELOW

SKYLIGHTS

SECOND FLR.

No. 19491

No. 19491

From the sheltered veranda to the connected active areas, this award-winning home says "Welcome". Look at the efficient U-shaped kitchen, with pass-through convenience that keeps the cook in the conversation around the dining table. Ceilings soar to dramatic heights in the adjoining living room. And, upstairs, the master loft with its own private deck provides a commanding view of the scene below, along with loads of built-in storage. With its own private bath and room-sized closet, this room will be a retreat you'll never want to leave. Tucked away from active areas, a roomy first floor bedroom and study flank a combined bath and laundry center.

First floor — 920 sq. ft.
Second floor — 300 sq. ft.
Garage — 583 sq. ft.

Total living area — 1,220 sq. ft.

A *ward*
Winning
Design

No. 19938

This two-story home is ideal for those on a budget looking for an adaptable design. The primary living areas on the lower floor complete the basic one-bedroom plan, leaving the upper level, breezeway and garage for completion later. The two rooms on the upper level could be used as bedrooms, a hobby room, private office, or almost anything you choose. The family-dining-living areas are open to the multi-purpose room above and only partially divided from one another, creating a more spacious and formal atmosphere. You're sure to find that this plan offers a lot for a little.

First floor — 1,090 sq. ft.
Second floor — 580 sq. ft.
Garage — 484 sq. ft.

Total living area — 1,670 sq. ft.

*A*daptable
**To Your
Needs**

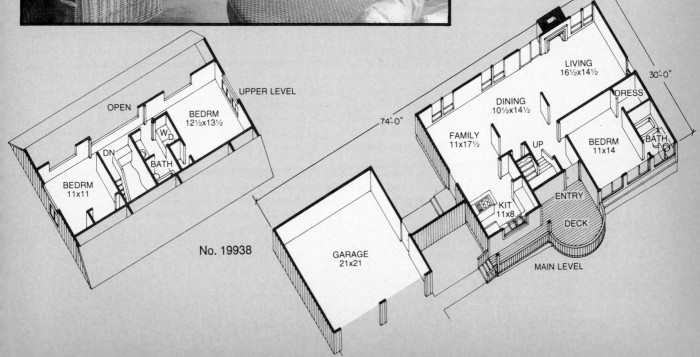

UPPER LEVEL

OPEN

BEDRM
12½x13½

W D

DN

BATH

BEDRM
11x11

No. 19938

LIVING
16½x14½

30'-0"

DINING
10½x14½

DRESS

74'-0"

FAMILY
11x17½

UP

BEDRM
11x14

BATH

KIT
11x8

ENTRY

DECK

GARAGE
21x21

MAIN LEVEL

Delightful Floor Plan Enhanced
with Many Amenities

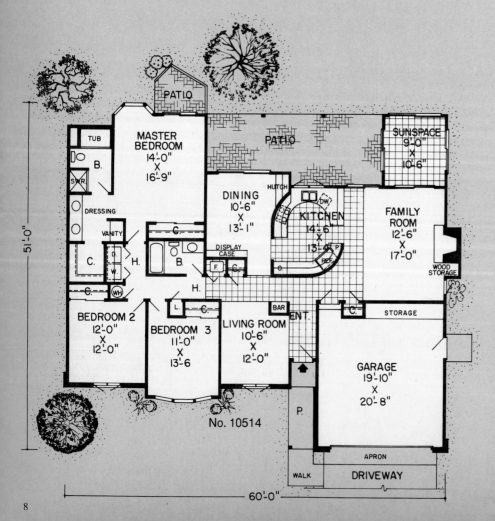

No. 10514

The unusual design of the kitchen provides the centerpiece for this thoroughly delightful floor plan. The kitchen is further enhanced by the tiled hallways which surround it and delineate the adjacent living areas. The dining room, which opens onto the patio with large glass doors, includes both a built-in hutch and a display case. The large family room has a fireplace with its own wood storage and provides direct access to the sunspace. The master bedroom suite has a private patio, bay window, five-piece bath, separate vanity and a large, walk-in closet.

Main living area — 1,954 sq. ft.
Garage — 448 sq. ft.
Sunroom — 144 sq. ft.

Total living area — 1,954 sq. ft.

Floor plan labels

PATIO

MASTER BEDROOM
14'-0"
X
16'-9"

TUB
B.
SWR.
DRESSING
VANITY
C.
H.
D
W
WH
C.

DINING
10'-6"
X
13'-1"

HUTCH

PATIO

KITCHEN
14'-6"
X
13'-4"

DW
REF.

DISPLAY CASE
F.
C.
H.
B.

SUNSPACE
9'-0"
X
10'-6"

FAMILY ROOM
12'-6"
X
17'-0"

WOOD STORAGE

BEDROOM 2
12'-0"
X
12'-0"

BEDROOM 3
11'-0"
X
13'-6

LIVING ROOM
10'-6"
X
12'-0"

BAR
ENT.

STORAGE

C.

GARAGE
19'-10"
X
20'-8"

P.

No. 10514

51'-0"

60'-0"

APRON
WALK
DRIVEWAY

Photography by Westerfield Studios

No. 20060

S'triking Angles...

Striking angles best describes this contemporary design. At the front entrance, an attractive half-circle window transom is built above the door. Through the foyer, the kitchen is centered perfectly between the breakfast area and a more formal dining area. The breakfast room leads onto a very large wooden deck through sliding glass doors. From the breakfast room, the living room comes complete with a wood-burning fireplace, plus the extra feature of a sloping, open-beamed ceiling. This design offers the master bedroom on the entry level, complete with a dressing area, walk-in closet, and full bath. The second level offers two bedrooms with a full bath and a convenient cedar closet.

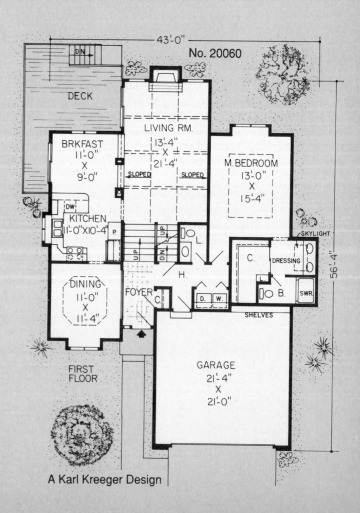

No. 20060

43'-0"

56'-4"

DECK

BRKFAST 11'-0" X 9'-0"

LIVING RM. 13'-4" X 21'-4"

SLOPED

M. BEDROOM 13'-0" X 15'-4"

DW

KITCHEN 11'-0"X10'-4"

SKYLIGHT

UP

DN

UP

C.

DRESSING

DINING 11'-0" X 11'-4"

FOYER

C.

D. W.

B.

SWR.

SHELVES

H.

FIRST FLOOR

GARAGE 21'-4" X 21'-0"

A Karl Kreeger Design

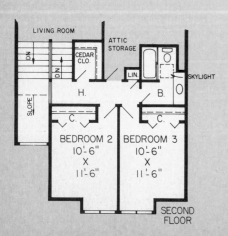

LIVING ROOM

ATTIC STORAGE

DN

CEDAR CLO.

LIN.

SKYLIGHT

SLOPE

H.

B.

C.

C.

BEDROOM 2 10'-6" X 11'-6"

BEDROOM 3 10'-6" X 11'-6"

SECOND FLOOR

Photography by Ingrid Smith

First floor — 1,279 sq. ft.
Second floor — 502 sq. ft.
Basement — 729 sq. ft.
Garage — 470 sq. ft.

Total living area — 1,781 sq. ft.

C'ontemporary Design

*E*legant Entrance to Impressive Home

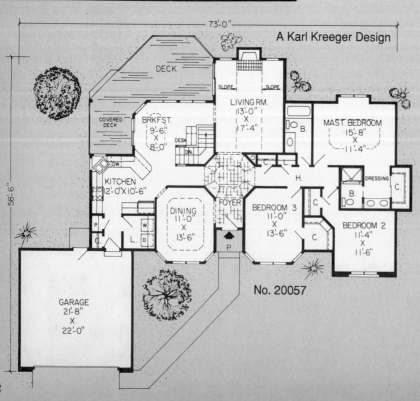

A Karl Kreeger Design

73'-0"

58'-6"

DECK

SLOPE   SLOPE

LIVING RM.
13'-0"
X
17'-4"

COVERED
DECK

BRKFST.
9'-6"
X
8'-0"

DESK
DN

B.

MAST. BEDROOM
15'-8"
X
11'-4"

DW

KITCHEN
12'-0"X10'-6"

H.

DRESSING
C.

P

C.

DINING
11'-0"
X
13'-6"

W
L.   D

FOYER

C.

B.

BEDROOM 3
11'-0"
X
13'-6"

C.

BEDROOM 2
11'-4"
X
11'-6"

P

No. 20057

GARAGE
21'-8"
X
22'-0"

No. 20057

Two copper-roofed bay windows and a stone veneer front create an elegant entrance through an attractive circle head transom. Enjoy the vaulted-ceilings that extend into the foyer, dining room, breakfast room, and master bedroom (with private dressing area). Even the kitchen is impressive with two separate eating areas and a connecting pantry for storage. Sliding glass doors from the breakfast room lead to a huge deck.

Main living area — 1,804 sq. ft.
Basement — 1,804 sq. ft.
Garage & workshop — 499 sq. ft.

Total living area — 1,804 sq. ft.

Photography by John Ehrenclou

Photography by Carren Strock

S'plit-Level Tudor Offers Comfort and Versatility

No. 10544

This contemporary Tudor-style design boasts features that make a house a home, including a master bedroom with a full bath, a spacious kitchen adjoining the formal dining room, and a fireplace in the large family room on the lower level. Step up to the three bedrooms situated separately from the rest of the living areas giving a sense of privacy for family or guests. The bay window in the dining room provides a bit of elegance for entertaining.

Upper levels — 1,366 sq. ft.
Lower level — 384 sq. ft.
Basement — 631 sq. ft.
Garage — 528 sq. ft.

Total living area — 1,750 sq. ft.

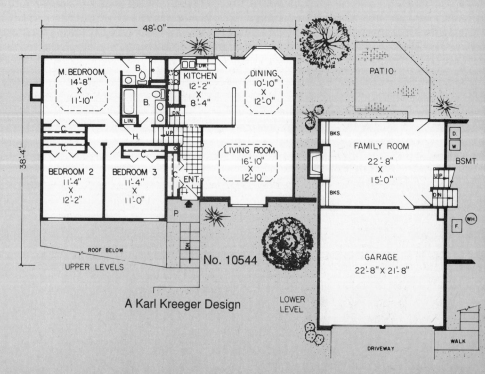

No. 10544

A Karl Kreeger Design

Photography by John Ehrenclou

C'overed Porch Offered in Farm-Type Traditional

No. 34901

This pleasant traditional design has a farmhouse flavor exterior that incorporates a covered porch and features a circle wood louver on its garage, giving this design a feeling of sturdiness. Inside on the first level to the right of the foyer is a formal dining room complete with a bay window, an elevated ceiling, and a corner china cabinet. To the left of the foyer is the living room with a wood-burning fireplace. The kitchen is connected to the breakfast room and there is also a room for the laundry facilities. A half-bath is also featured on the first floor. The second floor has three bedrooms. The master bedroom, on the second floor, has its own private bath and walk-in closet. The other two bedrooms share a full bath. A two-car garage is also added into this design.

First floor — 909 sq. ft.
Second floor — 854 sq. ft.
Basement — 899 sq. ft.
Garage — 491 sq. ft.

Total living area — 1,763 sq. ft.

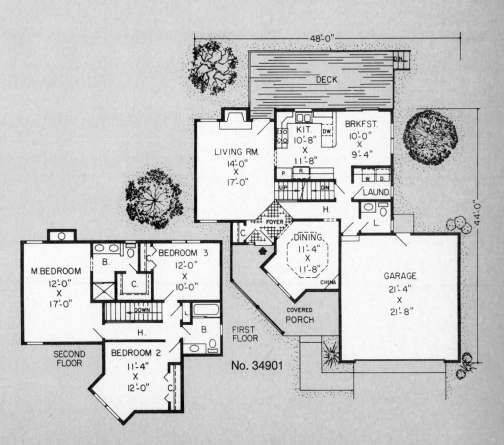

No. 34901

Railing Divides Living Spaces

No. 10596

This one-level design is a celebration of light and open space. From the foyer, view the dining room, island kitchen, breakfast room, living room, and outdoor deck in one sweeping glance. Bay windows add pleasing angles and lots of sunshine to eating areas and the master suite. And, a wall of windows brings the outdoors into the two back bedrooms.

Main living area — 1,740 sq. ft.
Basement — 1,377 sq. ft.
Garage — 480 sq. ft.

Total living area — 1,740 sq. ft.

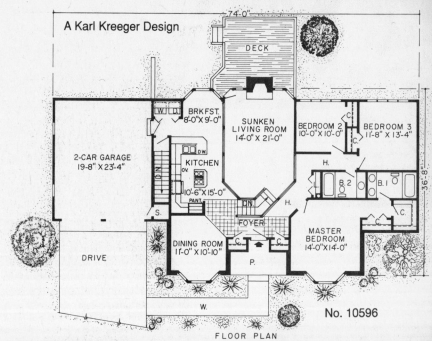

A Karl Kreeger Design

FLOOR PLAN

No. 10596

Carefree Convenience

No. 20402

Although this adaptable, one-level gem features handicapped accessibility, it's an excellent choice for anyone looking for an easy-care home. Notice the extra-wide hallways, the master bath with roll-in shower, and specially designed kitchen with roll-out pantry and counters designed for wheelchair access. A sunny, spacious atmosphere envelopes each room, thanks to generous windows and sloping ceilings. Reach the deck from the U-shaped kitchen overlooking the fireplaced family room, and from the master suite. The dining room and living room, separated by a handy bar and just steps away from the kitchen, are ideal for entertaining. A hall bath serves the front bedrooms.

Main living area — 2,153 sq. ft.
Garage — 617 sq. ft.
Porch — 210 sq. ft.

Total living area — 2,153 sq. ft.

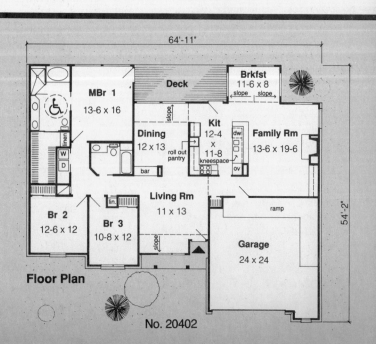

Floor Plan

No. 20402

Sloped-Ceiling is Attractive Feature

No. 10548

The fireplace and sloped-ceiling in the family room offer something a bit out of the ordinary in a small home. The master bedroom is complete with full bath and a dressing area. Bedrooms two and three share a full bath across the hall, and a half bath is conveniently located adjacent to the kitchen. A bump-out bay window is shown in the spacious breakfast room, and a bay window with window seat has been designed in the master bedroom. The screened porch off of the breakfast room is an inviting feature for meals outside.

Main living area — 1,688 sq. ft.
Basement — 1,688 sq. ft.
Screened porch — 120 sq. ft.
Garage — 489 sq. ft.

Total living area — 1,688 sq. ft.

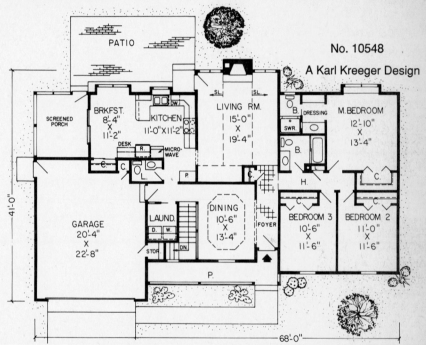

No. 10548

A Karl Kreeger Design

Stucco and Stone Reveal Outstanding Tudor Design

No. 10555

This beautiful stucco and stone masonry Tudor design opens to a formal foyer that leads through double doors into a well-designed library which is also conveniently accessible from the master bedroom. The master bedroom offers a vaulted ceiling and a huge bath area. Other features are an oversized living room with a fireplace, an open kitchen and a connecting dining room. A utility room and half-bath are located next to a two-car garage. One other select option in this design is the separate cedar closet to use for off-season clothes storage.

First floor — 1,671 sq. ft.
Second floor — 505 sq. ft.
Basement — 1,661 sq. ft.
Garage — 604 sq. ft.
Screened porch — 114 sq. ft.

Total living area — 2,176 sq. ft.

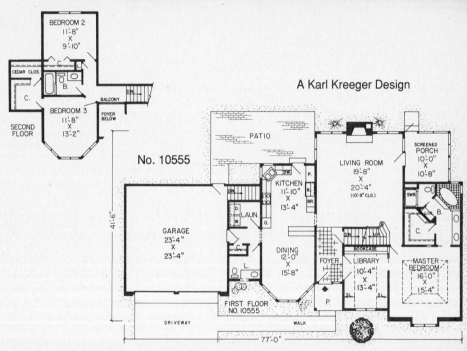

A Karl Kreeger Design

Easy Living

No. 20164

Here's a pretty, one-level home designed for carefree living. The central foyer divides active and quiet areas. Step back to a fireplaced living room with dramatic, towering ceilings and a panoramic view of the backyard. The adjoining dining room features a sloping ceiling crowned by a plant shelf, and sliders to an outdoor deck. Just across the counter, a handy, U-shaped kitchen features abundant cabinets, a window over the sink overlooking the deck, and a walk-in pantry. You'll find three bedrooms tucked off the foyer. Front bedrooms share a handy full bath, but the master suite boasts its own private bath with both shower and tub, a room-sized walk-in closet, and a bump-out window that adds light and space.

Main living area — 1,456 sq. ft.
Basement — 1,448 sq. ft.
Garage — 452 sq. ft.

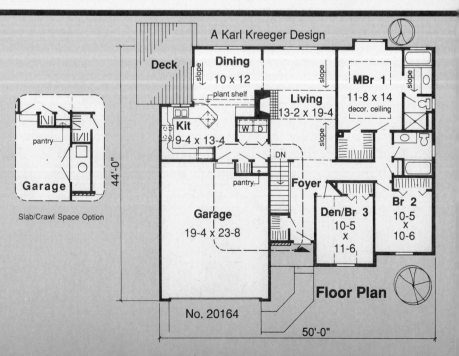

Slab/Crawl Space Option

18   **Total living area — 1,456 sq. ft.**

Dramatic Ranch

No. 20198

The exterior of this ranch home is all wood with interesting lines. More than an ordinary ranch home, it has a expansive feeling to drive up to. The large living area has a stone fireplace and decorative beams. The kitchen and dining room lead to an outside deck. The laundry room has a large pantry and is off the eating area. The master bedroom has a wonderful bathroom with a huge walk-in closet. In the front of the house there are two additional bedrooms with a bathroom. This house offers one-floor living and has nice big rooms.

Main living area — 1,792 sq. ft.
Basement — 864 sq. ft.
Garage — 928 sq. ft.

Total living area — 1,792 sq. ft.

56'-0"

No. 20198

A Karl Kreeger Design

Deck

Kitchen 12 x 11-4
Dining Rm 9 x 11-4
pantry
Ldry
MBr 1 14-2 x 14-4

32'-0"

Living Rm 21-6 x 19-4
decor. beams

Br 3 12 x 12-6
Br 2 12 x 12-6

Floor Plan

Compact Charmer Flooded with Sun

No. 20300

The clerestory window high over the covered porch of this inviting gem hints at the high excitement you'll find when you walk through the front door. From the soaring foyer to the sun room off the fireplaced living room and kitchen, this contemporary porch revival house is enveloped in warmth and sunlight. And, you'll find all the features you've been longing for: built in media and china cabinets, an efficient U-shaped kitchen, a central yet concealed first-floor powder room, a skylit master bath with double vanities, and three spacious bedrooms with loads of closet space.

First floor — 909 sq. ft.
Second floor —765 sq. ft.
Basement — 517 sq. ft.
Garage and stair — 479 sq. ft.

Total living area — 1,674 sq. ft.

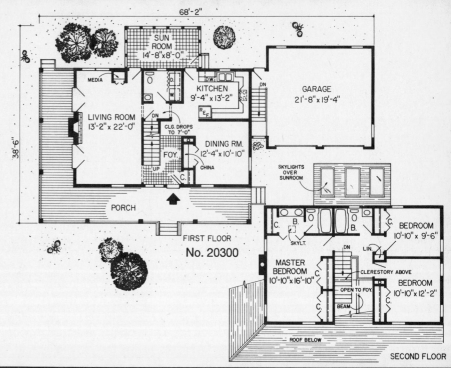

Stylish and Practical Plan

No. 20069

Make the most of daily life with a stylish yet practical plan. The garage and seldom-used formal dining room separate the main areas of the house from traffic noise, while the rear of the home maximizes comfort and livability. The kitchen contains a breakfast area large enough for most informal meals and serves snacks to the living room or deck equally well. The spacious living room is a joy in either summer or winter thanks to the fireplace and broad views of deck and backyard. All bedrooms have plenty of closet space, and you'll especially appreciate the attic storage.

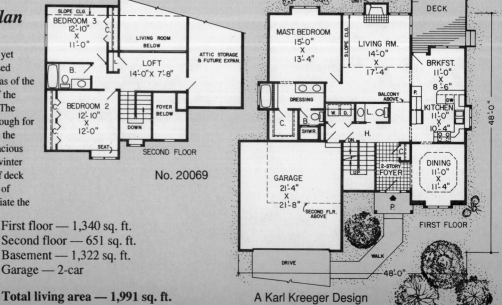

First floor — 1,340 sq. ft.
Second floor — 651 sq. ft.
Basement — 1,322 sq. ft.
Garage — 2-car

Total living area — 1,991 sq. ft.

A Karl Kreeger Design

Angular Design is Strikingly Contemporary

No. 10469

The living room is the focal point of this contemporary design and incorporates several innovative features. Its vaulted-ceiling is highlighted with exposed beams, and the angled front has up to four levels of windows which are operated by remote control. A wood-burning fireplace and built-in bookshelves enhance the rear wall of the room. The kitchen, informal serving area and dining room occupy the remainder of the first floor. The second floor is reserved for the three spacious bedrooms. The master bedroom also has a beamed-ceiling plus its own fireplace.

First floor — 989 sq. ft.
Second floor — 810 sq. ft.
Garage — 538 sq. ft.

Total living area — 1,799 sq. ft.

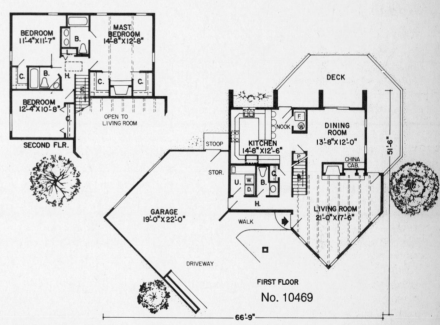

SECOND FLR.

BEDROOM
11'-4"x11'-7"

MAST. BEDROOM
14'-8"x12'-8"

BEDROOM
12'-4"x10'-8"

OPEN TO LIVING ROOM

FIRST FLOOR
No. 10469

DECK

KITCHEN
14'-8"x12'-6"

DINING ROOM
13'-8"x12'-0"

CHINA CAB.

LIVING ROOM
21'-0"x17'-6"

GARAGE
19'-0"x22'-0"

STOOP

STOR.

WALK

DRIVEWAY

51'-6"

66'-9"

Ranch Incorporates Victorian Features

No. 20058

This wonderful Victorian-featured ranch design incorporates many luxury conveniences usually offered in larger designs. The master bedroom is expansive, with an oversized full bath complete with a walk-in closet, an individual shower, a full tub, and a two-sink wash basin. A large kitchen area is offered with a built-in island for convenience. The kitchen also has its own breakfast area. Located next to the kitchen is a half-bath. The living area is separated from the dining room by a half-wall partition. Two large bedrooms complete the interior of the house. They have large closets and share a full bath. A two-car garage and a wood deck complete the options listed in this design.

Main living area — 1,787 sq. ft.
Basement — 1,787 sq. ft.
Garage — 484 sq. ft.

Total living area — 1,787 sq. ft.

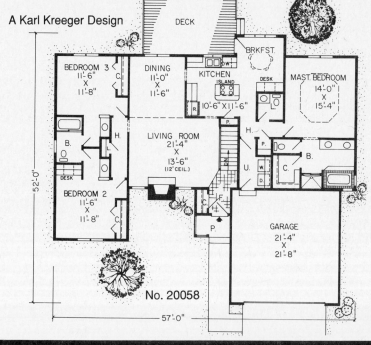

A Karl Kreeger Design

No. 20058

Lots of Living in Four-Bedroom Starter

No. 10520

This traditional exterior, with its charming dormers, provides four bedrooms and lots of style even on a small lot. The very large master suite on the second floor includes the luxury of a jacuzzi. The other second floor bedroom also has a private bath and a walk-in closet. On the first floor are two more bedrooms which share a bath. The living room is reminiscent of the old-fashioned parlor. The dining area and U-shaped kitchen are located toward the back of the house overlooking the lawn providing an ideal setting for family meals.

First floor — 960 sq. ft.
Second floor — 660 sq. ft.
Basement — 960 sq. ft.

Total living area — 1,620 sq. ft.

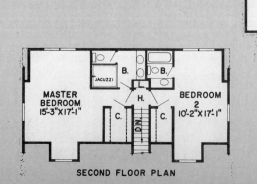

FIRST FLOOR PLAN
No. 10520

SECOND FLOOR PLAN

Green House Adds Charm and Warmth to Multi-Level Plan

No. 10468

The well-placed solar greenhouse is located on the lower level of this inviting design. Sliding glass doors open into the greenhouse from the family room while casement windows over the kitchen sink open into the space above. The master bedroom also has access to the outdoors through the sliding glass doors onto an elevated deck. Two additional bedrooms are located across the hall. The living room is warmed by a hearth fireplace and adjoins the combined kitchen and dining areas.

Upper level — 1,294 sq. ft.
Family room level — 292 sq. ft.
Garage — 608 sq. ft.
Greenhouse — 164 sq. ft.

Total living area — 1,586 sq. ft.

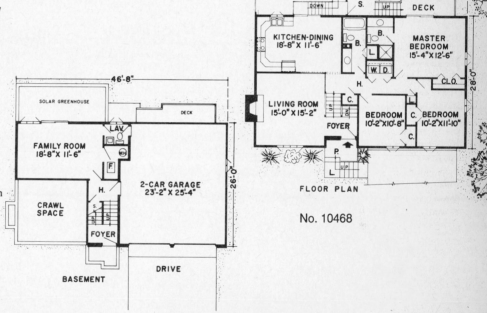

No. 10468

Enticing Two-Story Traditional

No. 34027

This beautiful home accommodates the needs of a growing family and looks stunning in any neighborhood. The porch serves as a wonderful relaxing area to enjoy the outdoors. At the rear of the home is a patio, for a barbeque or for more private time away from the kids. Inside is just as delightful. The dining room features a decorative ceiling and has easy entry to the kitchen. The kitchen/utility area has a side exit into the garage. The living room has double doors into the fireplaced family room which features a back entrance to the patio. Upstairs is the sleeping area with three bedrooms plus a vaulted-ceiling master bedroom. The master bedroom has two enormous walk-in closets, as well as a dressing area and private bath. Please specify slab, crawlspace or basement when ordering.

First floor — 925 sq. ft.
Second floor — 975 sq. ft.
Garage — 484 sq. ft.

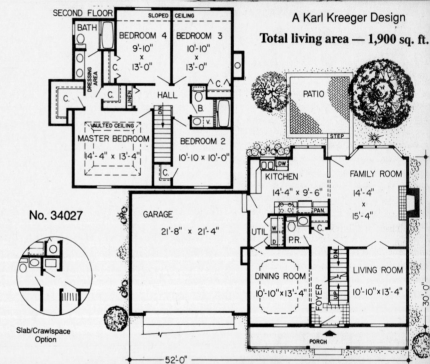

No. 34027

Slab/Crawlspace Option

SECOND FLOOR

A Karl Kreeger Design

Total living area — 1,900 sq. ft.

Cape Cod Passive Solar Design

No. 10386

A solar greenhouse on the south employs energy storage rods and water to capture the sun's warmth, thereby providing a sanctuary for plants and supplying a good percentage of the house's heat. Other southern windows are large and triple glazed for energy efficiency. From one of the bedrooms, on the second floor, you can look out through louvered shutters to the living room below, accented by a heat-circulating fireplace and a cathedral ceiling with three dormer windows which flood the room with light. On the lower level, sliding glass doors lead from the sitting area of the master bedroom suite to a private patio.

First floor — 1,164 sq. ft.
Second floor — 574 sq. ft.
Basement — 1,164 sq. ft.
Greenhouse — 238 sq. ft.
Garage & storage — 574 sq. ft.

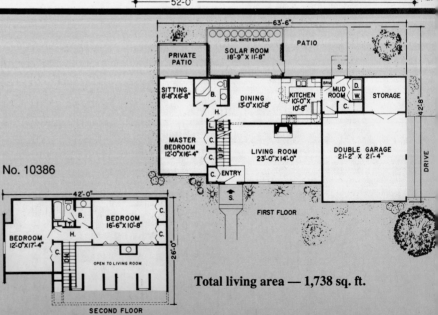

No. 10386

Total living area — 1,738 sq. ft.

Multi-Level Excitement

No. 20102

With abundant windows, a skylit breakfast room with sliders to a rear deck, and an open plan overlooking the sunken living room below, the foyer level of this distinctive home is a celebration of open space. You'll appreciate the step-saving design of the island kitchen that easily serves both dining rooms. And, you'll enjoy the warmth of the living room fireplace throughout the lower levels of the house. A stairway leads from the foyer to the bedroom level that houses the spacious master suite with a private bath, and two additional bedrooms served by a full bath. The lucky inhabitant of the fourth bedroom, tucked away at the top of the house, will love this private retreat overlooking the two floors below.

First level — 1,003 sq. ft.
Second level — 808 sq. ft.
Third level — 241 sq. ft.
Basement — 573 sq. ft.
Garage — 493 sq. ft.

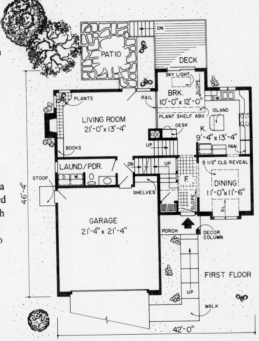

Total living area — 2,052 sq. ft.

No. 20102

A Karl Kreeger Design

Trim Plan Designed for Handicapped

No. 10360

Attractive and accessible, this three bedroom home has been carefully detailed to provide both comfort and self-sufficiency for the handicapped individual. Ramps allow entry to garage, patio and porch. Doors and windows are located so that they can be opened with ease, and both baths feature wall-hung toilets at a special 16-18" height. Spacious rooms, wide halls, and the oversized double garage allow wheel-chair to be maneuvered with minimal effort, and the sink and cooktop are also located with this in mind.

Main living area — 1,882 sq. ft.
Garage — 728 sq. ft.

Total living area — 1,882 sq. ft.

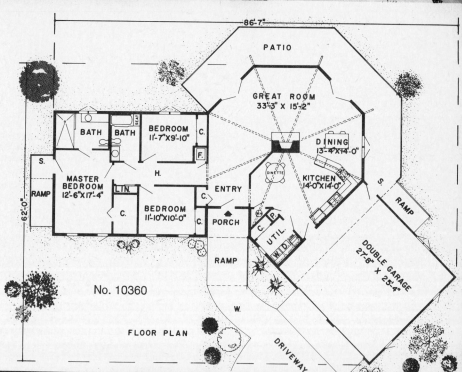

No. 10360

FLOOR PLAN

Intelligent Use of Space

No. 10483

Lots of living is packed into this well-designed home which features a combined kitchen and dining room. The highly functional U-shaped kitchen includes a corner sink under double windows. Opening onto the dining room is the living room which is illuminated by both a front picture window and a skylight. Its lovely fireplace makes this an inviting place to gather. The sleeping area of this home contains three bedrooms and two full baths, one of which is a private bath accessed only from the master bedroom.

Main living area — 1,025 sq. ft.
Garage — 403 sq. ft.

Total living area — 1,025 sq. ft.

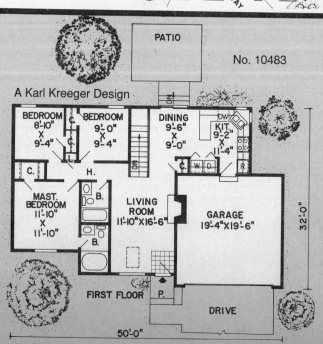

No. 10483

A Karl Kreeger Design

FIRST FLOOR

Ranch Style Favors Living Room

No. 6360

Stretching over 22 feet to span the width of this ranch design, the living room is indulged with expanses of windows, a wood-burning fireplace, and access to the terrace. A separate, well-windowed dining room and an efficient kitchen with abundant counter space border the living room. Three bedrooms complete this plan.

Main living area — 1,342 sq. ft.
Basement — 767 sq. ft.
Garage — 466 sq. ft.
Terrace — 92 sq. ft.

Total living area — 1,342 sq. ft.

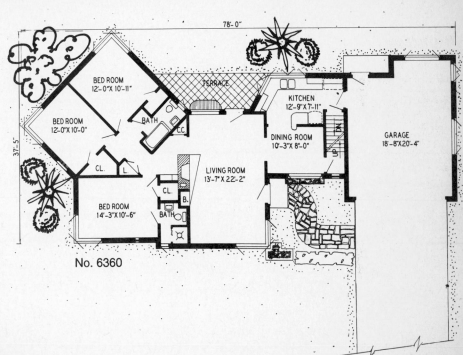

No. 6360

Distinctive Living

No. 8266

You'll enjoy this combination of an attractive exterior and a most convenient and livable interior. There are three large bedrooms and two full baths. The living room shows an interior wall fireplace. The modern built-in kitchen is flanked to the left by the dining room and on the right by a dinette. Note the siding and the folding doors between the kitchen, the dining room and living room. A stairway leads to the basement which provides more utility space as well as future recreational areas.

Main living area — 1,604 sq. ft.
Garage — 455 sq. ft.
Basement — 1,604 sq. ft.

Total living area — 1,604 sq. ft.

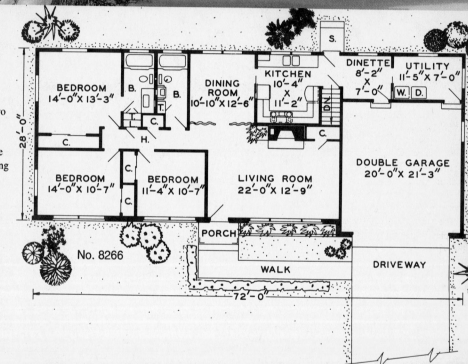

Fireplace is a Special Feature

No. 9838

Family convenience is emphasized in this beautiful ranch style home. The owner's suite includes double closets and a private bath with a spacious built-in vanity. A two-way wood-burning fireplace between the living room and dining room permits the fire to be enjoyed from both rooms. An extra large garage possesses an abundance of extra storage space.

Main living area — 1,770 sq. ft.
Basement — 1,770 sq. ft.
Garage — 700 sq. ft.

Total living area — 1,770 sq. ft.

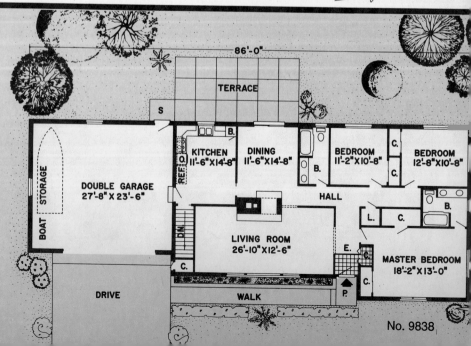

Fireplace in Living and Family Rooms

No. 9263

This beautiful ranch design features an extra large living room with plenty of formal dining space at the opposite end. Large wood burning fireplaces are found in both the living and family rooms. A mudroom, located off the kitchen, features a laundry area, half bath and storage closet. The charming master bedroom has a full bath and plenty of closet space.

Main living area — 1,878 sq. ft.
Garage — 538 sq. ft.

Total living area — 1,878 sq. ft.

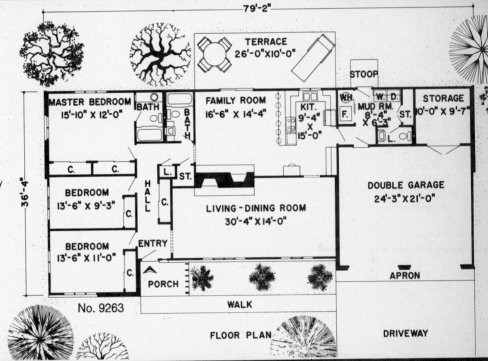

79'-2"

36'-4"

TERRACE
26'-0"X10'-0"

STOOP

MASTER BEDROOM
15'-10" X 12'-0"

BATH

BATH

FAMILY ROOM
16'-6" X 14'-4"

KIT.
9'-4"
X
15'-0"

W.H.
F.

W. D.
MUD RM.
8'-4"
X 6'-3"
L.

ST.

STORAGE
10'-0" X 9'-7"

C.   C.

BEDROOM
13'-6" X 9'-3"

C.

HALL

L. ST.

C.

LIVING - DINING ROOM
30'-4" X14'-0"

DOUBLE GARAGE
24'-3" X 21'-0"

BEDROOM
13'-6" X 11'-0"

ENTRY

C.

PORCH

APRON

No. 9263

WALK

FLOOR PLAN

DRIVEWAY

Compact Plans Offers Lots of Living Space

No. 10502

This three bedroom home, with its interesting exterior roof lines, opens to a well-designed family floor plan. Two bedrooms are separated on the second level while the master suite is secluded on the first floor. The master suite includes a five-piece bath with double vanity plus a full-wall closet. The remainder of the first floor encompasses a spacious living room complete with sloped-ceiling, a hearth fireplace and double windows. The dining room enlarges the living room and adjoins the U-shaped kitchen which is separated from the sunny breakfast room by a bar. The deck area provides a lovely area for outdoor family gatherings.

First floor — 1,172 sq. ft.
Second floor — 482 sq. ft.
Garage — 483 sq. ft.

Total living area — 1,654 sq. ft.

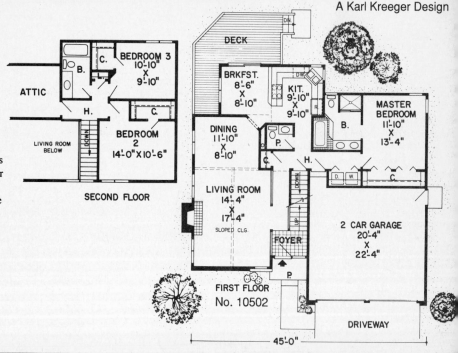

A Karl Kreeger Design

FIRST FLOOR
No. 10502

SECOND FLOOR

Greenhouse Brightens Compact Home

No. 20053

The kitchen features breakfast space, a built-in desk, pantry and a compact laundry area. Also on the first floor is the master bedroom with its private, five-piece bath. Both the entry foyer and the living room are open to the second floor creating a bridge between the two second floor bedrooms. In addition to the second floor's two bedrooms, full bath and linen closet, there is access to a large storage area under the eaves.

First floor — 1,088 sq. ft.
Second floor — 451 sq. ft.
Greenhouse — 72 sq. ft.
Garage — 473 sq. ft.

Total living area — 1,539 sq. ft.

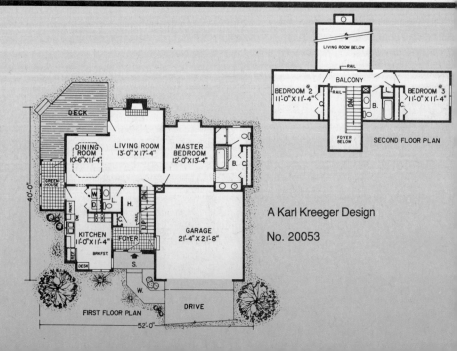

A Karl Kreeger Design

No. 20053

SECOND FLOOR PLAN

FIRST FLOOR PLAN

Simple Yet Elegant Lines Enclose Livable Plan

No. 10484

This two-story home offers integrated living spaces for an active family. The front breakfast room is just across the counter from the efficiently organized kitchen which is highlighted by a bump-out window over the double sink. Neatly tucked between the kitchen and breakfast room is the laundry center. Adjacent to the kitchen is the dining room which flows into the living room and the warmth of its hearth fireplace. Upstairs are three bedrooms including a generous master suite.

First floor — 869 sq. ft.
Second floor — 840 sq. ft.
Basement — 869 sq. ft.
Garage — 440 sq. ft.

Total living area — 1,709 sq. ft.

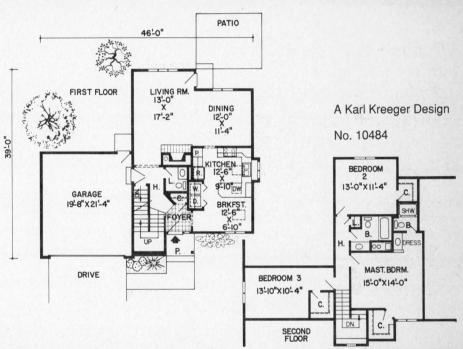

A Karl Kreeger Design

No. 10484

Master Suite Crowns Plan

No. 10394

The master bedroom suite occupies the entire second level of this passive solar design. The living room rises two stories in the front, as does the foyer, and can be opened to the master suite to aid in air circulation. Skylights in the sloping ceilings of the kitchen and master bath give abundant light to these areas. Angled walls, both inside and out, lend a unique appeal. An air lock entry, 2x6 exterior studs, 6-inch concrete floor, and generous use of insulation help make this an energy efficient design.

First floor — 1,306 sq. ft.
Second floor — 472 sq. ft.
Garage — 576 sq. ft.

Total living area — 1,778 sq. ft.

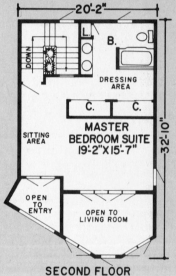

SECOND FLOOR

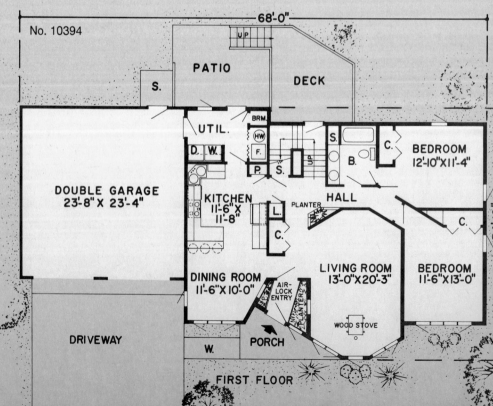

FIRST FLOOR

Wide-Open and Convenient

No. 20100

Stacked windows fill the wall in the front bedroom of this one-level home, creating an attractive facade, and a sunny atmosphere inside. Around the corner, two more bedrooms and two full baths complete the bedroom wing, set apart for bedtime quiet. Notice the elegant vaulted-ceiling in the master bedroom, the master tub and shower illuminated by a skylight, and the double vanities in both baths. Active areas enjoy a spacious feeling. Look at the high, sloping ceilings in the fireplaced living room, the sliders that unite the breakfast room and kitchen with an adjoining deck, and the vaulted-ceilings in the formal dining room off the foyer.

Main living area —
1,727 sq. ft.

Basement — 1,727 sq. ft.

Garage — 484 sq. ft.

**Total living area —
1,727 sq. ft**

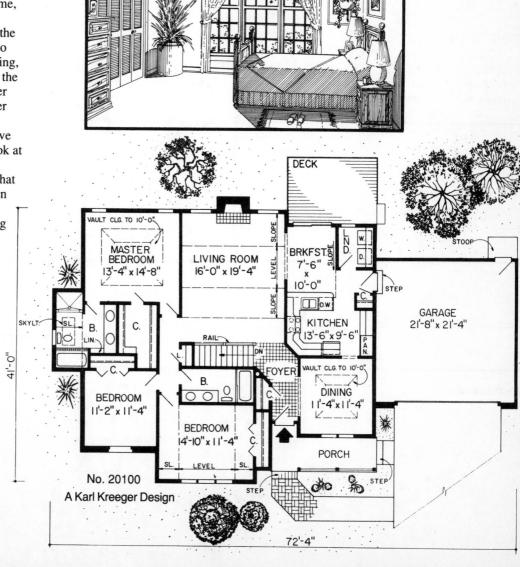

No. 20100

A Karl Kreeger Design

High Impact Angles

No. 90357

Lots of glass and soaring ceilings give this house a spacious, contemporary flavor in a compact space. A step down from the front entry, the fireplaced Great room adjoins a convenient kitchen with a sunny breakfast nook. Sliding glass doors open to an angular deck. Three bedrooms, located at the rear of the house to offer protection from street sounds, include a luxurious, vaulted-master suite with private bath.

Main living area — 1,368 sq. ft.
Garage — 2-car

Total living area —
1,368 sq. ft.

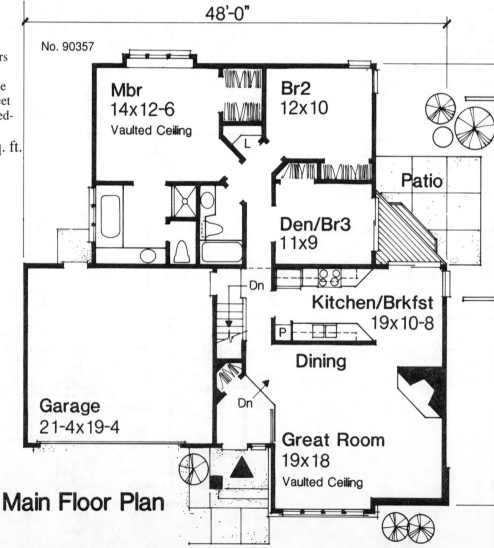

48'-0"

No. 90357

Mbr
14x12-6
Vaulted Ceiling

Br2
12x10

Patio

Den/Br3
11x9

Dn

Kitchen/Brkfst
19x10-8

Dining

Garage
21-4x19-4

Dn

Great Room
19x18
Vaulted Ceiling

Main Floor Plan

Bridge Adds Interior Drama

No. 20059

An upstairs bridge overlooks the foyer and living room in this dynamic design. Both the living and dining rooms have access to the rear deck. The kitchen has an adjoining breakfast area and a large pantry. The master bedroom has a spacious bath and walk-in closet. The other two bedrooms and bath are located on the second floor.

First floor — 1,293 sq. ft.
Second floor — 560 sq. ft.
Basement — 1,265 sq. ft.
Garage — 477 sq. ft.

Total living area — 1,853 sq. ft.

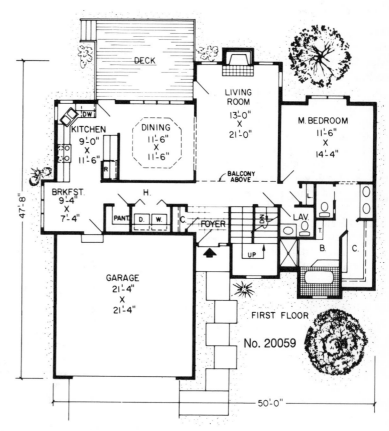

A Karl Kreeger Design

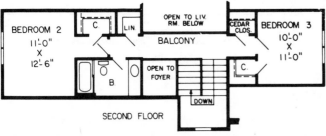

Super Starter

No. 10791

This affordable plan will let you have your house now, and keep your building budget in check. The entry opens to a spacious living room brightenened by a triple window arrangement. Step back to an open kitchen and dining room combination that features sliding glass doors to the back yard. The side entry, opposite the basement stairway, is handy when the kids come in from an afternoon of play. Prefer to save on foundation costs? Build the alternate crawlspace plan and separate the kitchen and breakfast nook with counters and cabinets. A hallway off the living room keeps the three bedrooms away from the action. Each features ample closet space and easy access to the large, hall bath.

Main living area — 1,092 sq. ft.

Total living area — 1,092 sq. ft.

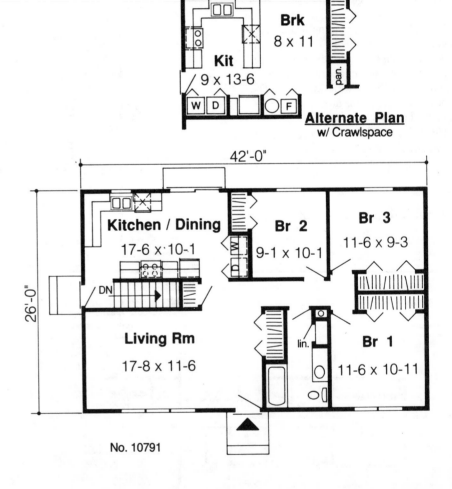

No. 10791

Delightful, Compact Home

No. 34003

Hanging plants would make for a magnificent entrance to this charming home. Walk into the fireplaced living room brightened by a wonderful picture window. The kitchen and dining area are separated by a counter island featuring double sinks. In the hallway, toward the bedrooms are a linen closet and full bath. The master bedroom features its own private bath and double closets. The two other bedrooms have good-sized closets, keeping clutter to a minimum. Many windows throughout this home lighten up each room, creating a warm, cozy atmosphere. Please indicate slab, crawl space or basement foundation when ordering.

Main living area — 1,146 sq. ft.

Total living area — 1,146 sq. ft.

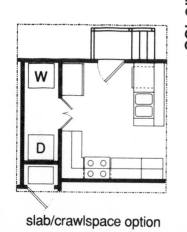

slab/crawlspace option

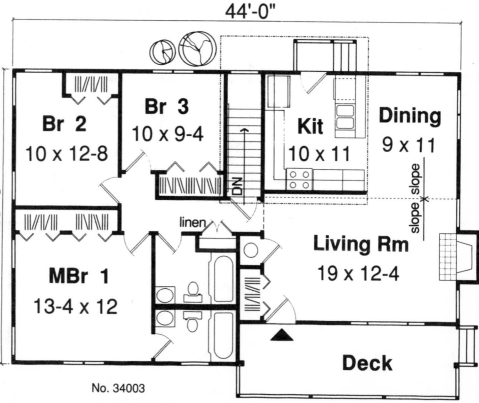

44'-0"

28'-0"

Br 2
10 x 12-8

Br 3
10 x 9-4

Kit
10 x 11

Dining
9 x 11

DN

linen

slope   slope

MBr 1
13-4 x 12

Living Rm
19 x 12-4

Deck

No. 34003

Easy Access; Easy Living

No. 99338

The living and dining rooms access a large deck, inviting outdoor meals and entertaining. The massive fireplace is flanked on each side by windows creating spectacular landscape views. A columned arcade divides living and dining areas. The bedroom off the front entrance might serve well as a den or office. The vaulted master suite includes walk-in wardrobe, luxurious spa bathing, and access to the deck.

Main living area — 1,642 sq. ft.
Basement — 1,642 sq. ft.
Garage — 2-car

Total living area — 1,642 sq. ft.

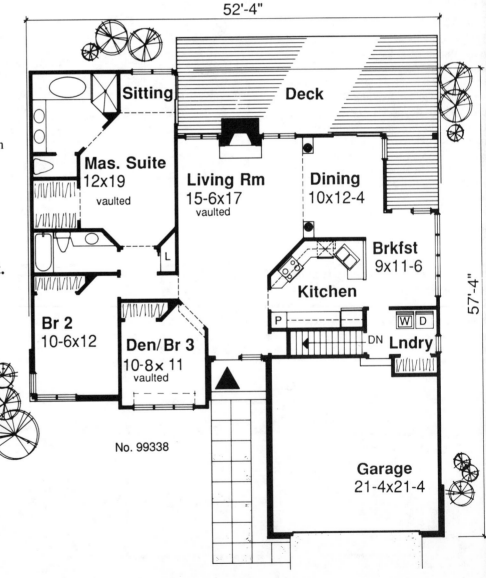

Zoned for Privacy

No. 91217

Don't worry about compromising your privacy in this one-level beauty. This plan is zoned to keep active and quiet areas separate. Step down from the foyer to a wide-open living room that flows into the formal dining room. Cathedral ceilings add to the spacious feeling that continues throughout active areas with an island kitchen open to the breakfast room. French doors lead from the kitchen to a screened porch, a nice warm-weather spot for your morning coffee. Down a hallway off the living room lie three bedrooms, each with a unique character. Notice how closets provide a separation from the bustle of active areas. And, with two full baths, even the morning rush shouldn't be a problem in this house. No materials list available for this plan.

Main living area — 1,811 sq. ft.
Screened porch — 121 sq. ft.
Garage — 437 sq. ft.

Total living area — 1,811 sq. ft.

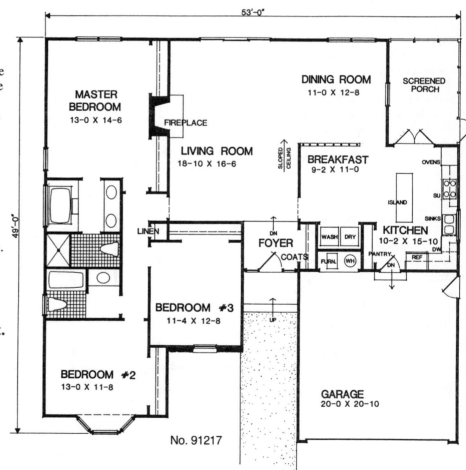

Storage Space
Galore in Garage

No. 20065

This simple design's exterior features a
large picture window and rock front.
On the first floor from the foyer is a
spacious living room with its own
wood-burning fireplace. The dining
room lies in front of the living room
and next to the kitchen. From the
kitchen to the right is the breakfast
room with access to a large outdoor
wooden deck. A half bath and laundry
facilities are other rooms on the first
floor. On the second floor are three
bedrooms. Two bedrooms share a full
bath with its own skylight, while the
master bedroom has its own private
bath and walk-in closet. One final
feature of this plan is the large amount
of storage space available in the two-
car garage.

First floor — 936 sq. ft.
Second floor — 777 sq. ft.
Garage/storage — 624 sq. ft.

Total living area — 1,713 sq. ft.

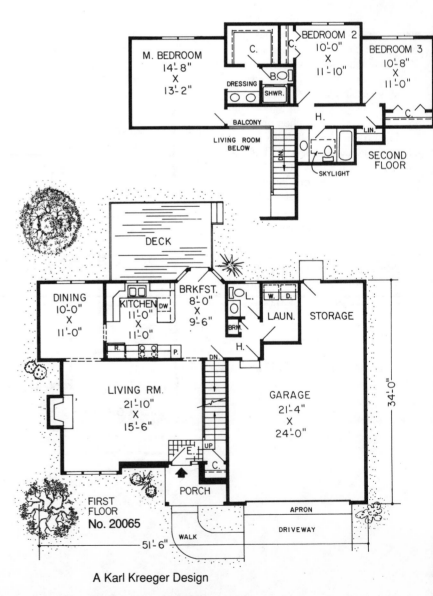

A Karl Kreeger Design

Comfortable Contemporary Design

No. 10567

This simple but well designed contemporary expresses comfort and offers a lot of options normally found in larger designs. On the first level, a front kitchen is offered with an open, non-partitioned dining area. Two bedrooms are located on the first floor. The living room sports a skylight, adding more natural lighting to the room, and has a pre-fabricated wood-burning fireplace. The second floor has a secluded master bedroom with a sitting room, walk-in closets, and a full bath. Other features include a two-car garage and a brick patio.

First floor — 1,046 sq. ft.
Second floor — 375 sq. ft.
Basement — 1,046 sq. ft.
Garage — 472 sq. ft.

Total living area — 1,421 sq. ft.

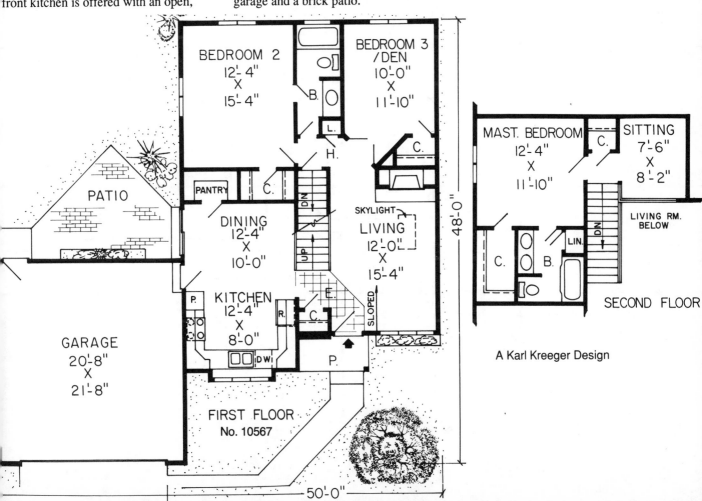

BEDROOM 2
12'-4" X 15'-4"

BEDROOM 3 /DEN
10'-0" X 11'-10"

PATIO

PANTRY

DINING
12'-4" X 10'-0"

LIVING
12'-0" X 15'-4"

SKYLIGHT

KITCHEN
12'-4" X 8'-0"

GARAGE
20'-8" X 21'-8"

FIRST FLOOR
No. 10567

50'-0"

48'-0"

MAST. BEDROOM
12'-4" X 11'-10"

SITTING
7'-6" X 8'-2"

LIVING RM. BELOW

SECOND FLOOR

A Karl Kreeger Design

Wonderful Views Everywhere

No. 20068

Consider this home if your backyard is something special in each season. Both living and dining areas offer broad views across the deck to the beautiful scene beyond. Even the balcony on the second floor captures it all. The open floor plan in the interior of the home brings the view to the kitchen and front hall as well. The master bedroom, with a fabulous walk-in closet and lavish bath, maintains its privacy to the side while indulging in the view of the backyard. The second floor bedrooms are notable for the huge closets.

First floor — 1,266 sq. ft.
Second floor — 489 sq. ft.
Basement — 1,266 sq. ft.
Garage — 484 sq. ft.

Total living area — 1,755 sq. ft.

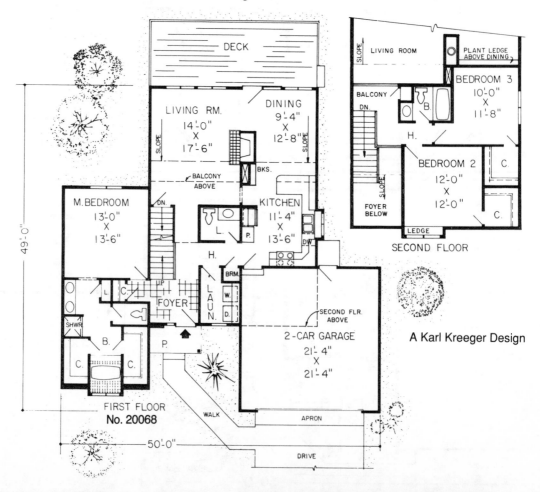

A Karl Kreeger Design

Gorgeous and Livable

No. 20196

This Karl Kreeger design has a look of luxury and a functional floor plan. The exterior is unique with its arched and octagon windows. The pillars give the porch a gracious, yet homey feel. The interior flows well because the living room and dining room are close together and just off the foyer which is quite spacious. The breakfast room is sunny and has an incredible shape. The family room has a fireplace and bar. The dining room has a decorative ceiling and overlooks the outside deck. The upstairs has a fantastic master bedroom suite, three additional bedrooms with bath and a convenient laundry room. The upstairs balcony is open to the downstairs and includes a plant shelf. The garage holds three cars.

First floor — 1,273 sq. ft.
Second floor — 1,477 sq. ft.
Basement — 974 sq. ft.
Garage — 852 sq. ft.

Total living area — 2,750 sq. ft.

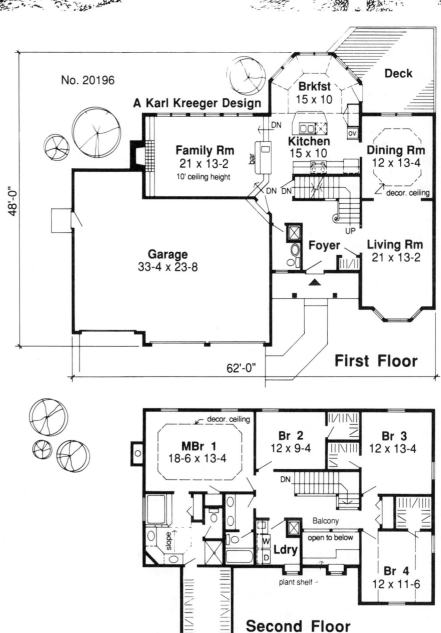

No. 20196

A Karl Kreeger Design

Deck

Brkfst 15 x 10

Kitchen 15 x 10

Dining Rm 12 x 13-4
decor. ceiling

Family Rm 21 x 13-2
10' ceiling height

Garage 33-4 x 23-8

Foyer

Living Rm 21 x 13-2

UP

48'-0"

62'-0"

First Floor

decor. ceiling

MBr 1 18-6 x 13-4

Br 2 12 x 9-4

Br 3 12 x 13-4

slope

DN

Ldry

Balcony open to below

plant shelf

Br 4 12 x 11-6

Second Floor

Good Things Come in Small Packages

No. 20303

Do you have a small lot, or a limited budget? Here's a compact gem that won't break the bank, and provides plenty of room for the whole family. And, this distinctive plan is an energy saver, too. Look at the air-lock vestibule entry that keeps the chill outside, and the skylights in both baths that let the sun help with the heating bills. There's a cozy sitting nook in the living room. A matching nook off the kitchen is a perfect spot for family meals. To insure quiet bedtimes, the central staircase separates the downstairs bedrooms from active areas. But for maximum privacy, escape upstairs to the master suite, which features double vanities, as well as a walk-in shower and tub.

First floor — 861 sq. ft.
Second floor — 333 sq. ft.
Basement — 715 sq. ft.

Total living area — 1,194 sq. ft.

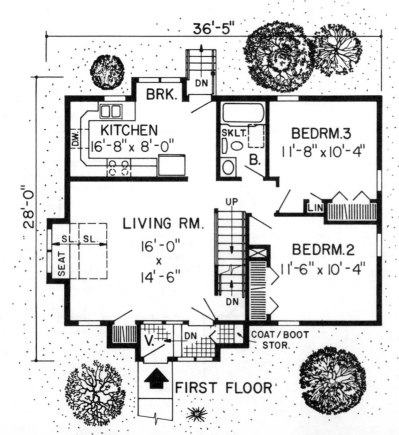

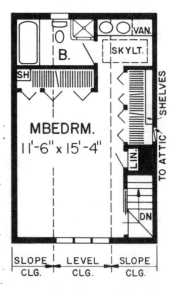

First-Time Owner's Delight

No. 20063

A distinctive exterior of wood veneer siding with a large, picture window combines with just a touch of brick to set this simple one-and-a-half story design into a class of its own. On the first level, the foyer leads directly into the living room which has a fireplace and is open to the dining room. The kitchen lies just to the left of the dining room. A laundry room is conveniently placed between the kitchen and the garage. The master bedroom lies on the first floor and has a full bath and walk-in closet. On the second floor two more bedrooms exist and share a full bath. There is also a loft area open to the living room below.

First floor — 1,161 sq. ft.
Second floor — 631 sq. ft.
Garage — 2-car

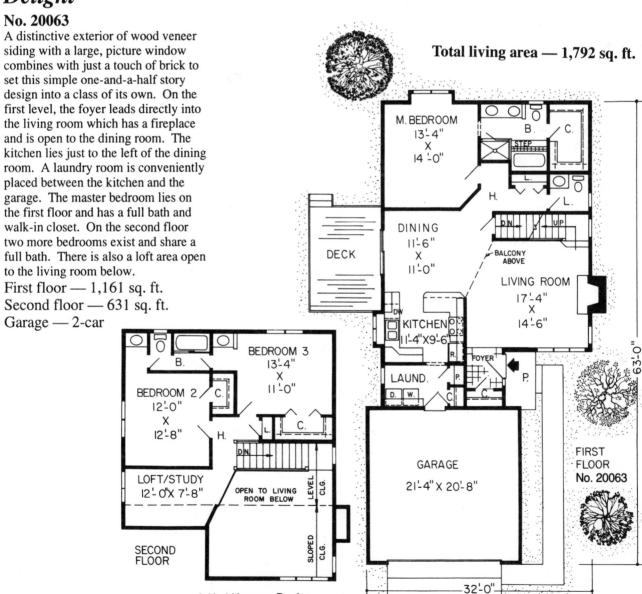

Total living area — 1,792 sq. ft.

M. BEDROOM
13'-4"
X
14'-0"

B.

C.

STEP

DINING
11'-6"
X
11'-0"

DECK

BALCONY ABOVE

LIVING ROOM
17'-4"
X
14'-6"

KITCHEN
11'-4" X 9'-6"

FOYER

LAUND.

63'-0"

GARAGE
21'-4" X 20'-8"

FIRST FLOOR
No. 20063

32'-0"

BEDROOM 3
13'-4"
X
11'-0"

B.

BEDROOM 2
12'-0"
X
12'-8"

C.

H.

LOFT/STUDY
12'-0" X 7'-8"

OPEN TO LIVING
ROOM BELOW

LEVEL CLG.

SLOPED CLG.

SECOND FLOOR

A Karl Kreeger Design

Coved Ceilings
Accent Design

No. 91644

A striking roofline and aristocratic profile serve notice to all that the days of fine living have not passed. The interior is designed with todays busy professional in mind. Compactness with no sacrifice of luxury. Coved ceilings, ample closet space and wrap-around kitchen. With a cozy fireplace in the living room it's just what the doctor ordered after a busy day at the office.
Main living area — 1,687 sq. ft.

Total living area — 1,687 sq. ft.

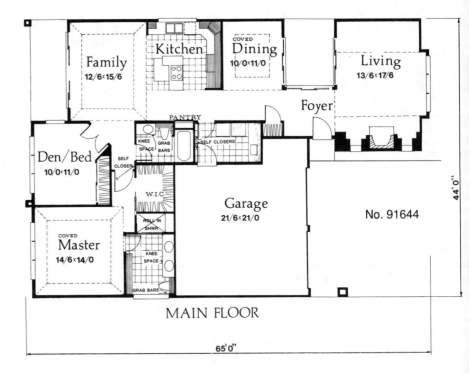

Family
12/6×15/6

Kitchen

COVED
Dining
10/0×11/0

Living
13/6×17/6

Foyer

PANTRY

KNEE SPACE   GRAB BARS

SELF CLOSERS

Den/Bed
10/0×11/0

SELF CLOSER

W.I.C.

ROLL IN SHWR

Garage
21/6×21/0

No. 91644

COVED
Master
14/6×14/0

KNEE SPACE

GRAB BARS

MAIN FLOOR

44'0"

65'0"

Spacious Kitchen Completes Special Design

No. 91654

This home has it all... beauty, luxury and livability. Marvel at the coved ceilings, large picture windows, and graciously curved staircase. Enjoy the luxury and unwind in front of the fireplace in the family or living room, or languish in the spa in the spacious master suite. This home also boasts a large U-shaped kitchen centered around a complete cooking island; a formal dining room for family and friends; three bathrooms; a bonus room; and optional upper floor.

Main floor — 1,233 sq. ft.
Upper floor — 902 sq. ft.
Bonus room — 168 sq. ft.

Total living area — 2,135 sq. ft.

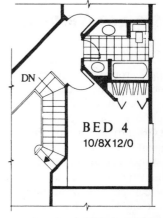

OPTIONAL UPPER FLOOR

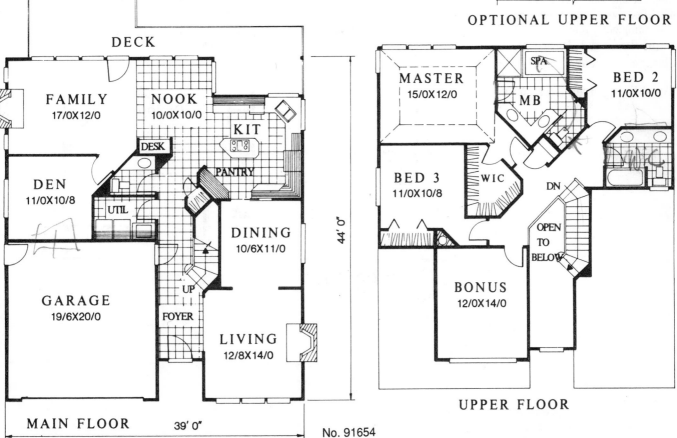

Nostalgia Returns

No. 99321

The return to nostalgic exterior
envelopes around contemporary
volumetric interior spaces of the late
80's is reflected in this appealing 1,368
square foot ranch design. The half-
round Great room transom window
with quarter round detail makes for an
interesting focal point inside and out.
The vaulted ceilings inside make the
rooms feel spacious, while the corner
fireplace and side deck through the
breakfast room sliders create an
interesting entry impact.

Main floor — 1,368 sq. ft.
Garage — 2-car

Total living area — 1,368 sq. ft.

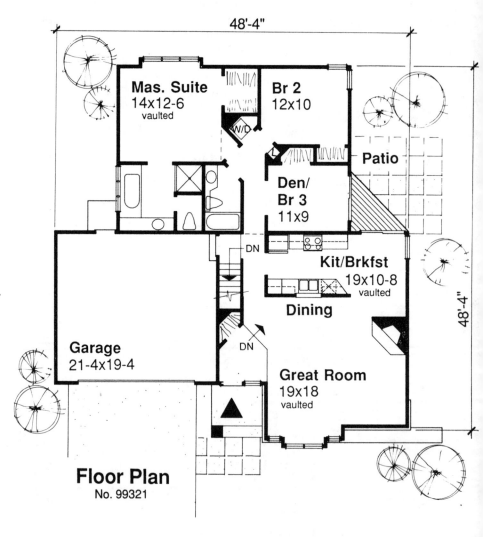

48'-4"

48'-4"

Mas. Suite
14x12-6
vaulted

Br 2
12x10

W/D

Patio

Den/
Br 3
11x9

DN

Kit/Brkfst
19x10-8
vaulted

Dining

Garage
21-4x19-4

DN

Great Room
19x18
vaulted

Floor Plan
No. 99321

Options Abound

No. 20061

This striking exterior features vertical siding, shake shingles, and rock, to set off a large picture window. Inside, the kitchen has a built-in pantry, refrigerator, dishwasher and range, breakfast bar, an open-beamed ceiling with a skylight, plus a breakfast area with lots of windows. A formal dining room complements the living room, which has two open beams running down a sloped-ceiling and a wood-burning fireplace. There is a laundry closet, and the foyer area also has a closet. Three bedrooms share a full bath. The master bedroom has an open-beamed, sloped-ceiling with a spacious bath area and a walk-in closet.

Main living area — 1,674 sq. ft.
Basement — 1,656 sq. ft.
Garage — 472 sq. ft.

Total living area — 1,674 sq. ft.

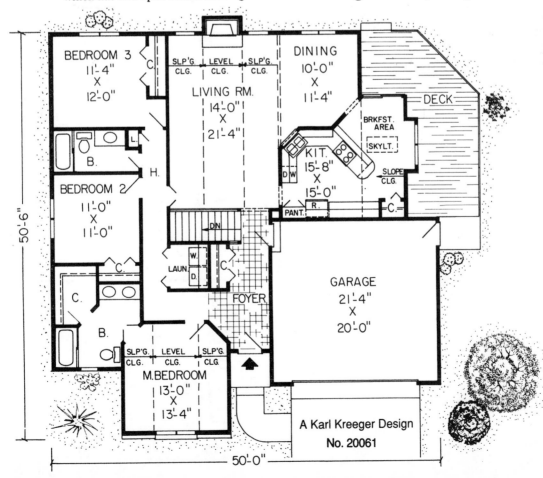

Convertible Charm

No. 91500

The compact footprint of this three-bedroom charmer makes it an ideal choice for the homebuilder on a budget, but its wide-open plan keeps the walls from closing in. Step inside the entry to a dramatic living and dining room that rises two stories. The living room fireplace adds a cozy feeling to both rooms. At the rear of the house, you'll find a well appointed kitchen convenient to both dining and family rooms. Upstairs, three bedrooms and two baths feature ample closet space and intriguing shapes that offer great decorating possibilities. The master suite is especially inviting, with its vaulted ceiling, double-vanitied bath, and huge window overlooking the backyard.

First floor — 748 sq. ft.
Second floor — 720 sq. ft.
Garage — 2-car

Total living area — 1,468 sq. ft.

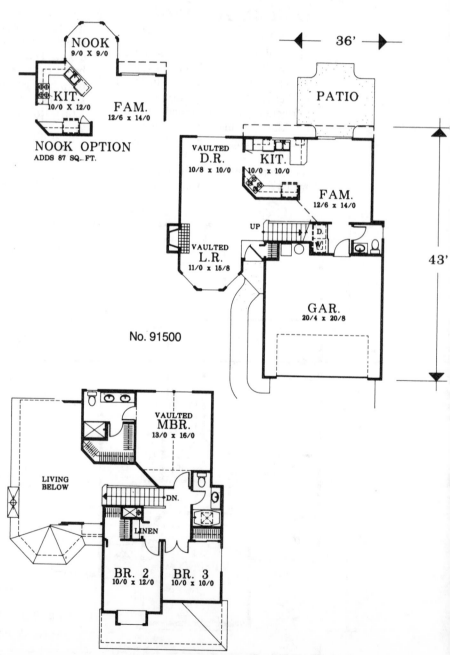

Balcony Overlooks Living Room Below

No. 90356

Smaller houses are getting better all the time, not only in their exterior character and scale, but in their use of spacial volumes and interior finish materials. Here a modest two-story gains importance, impact, and perceived value from the sweeping roof lines that make it look larger than it really is. Guests will be impressed by the impact of the vaulted ceiling in the living room up to the balcony hall above, the easy flow of traffic, and space in the kitchen and dining areas. Note too, the luxurious master bedroom suite with a window seat bay, walk-in closet, dressing area, and private shower.

Main floor — 674 sq. ft.
Upper floor — 677 sq. ft.
Garage — 2-car

Total living area — 1,351 sq. ft.

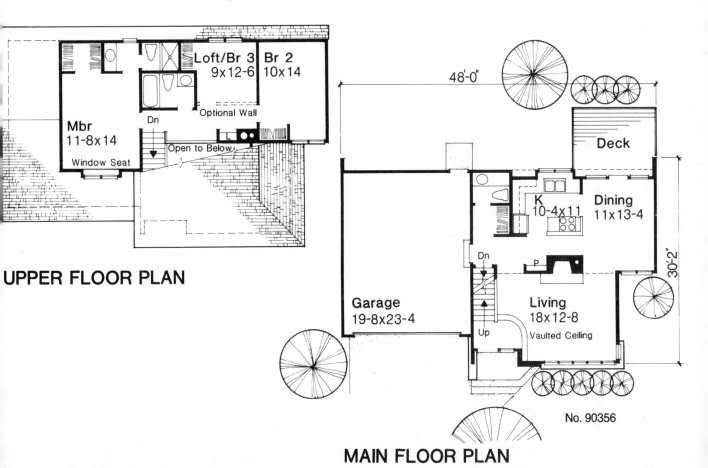

UPPER FLOOR PLAN

Loft/Br 3
9x12-6

Br 2
10x14

Optional Wall

Mbr
11-8x14

Window Seat

Dn

Open to Below

48'-0"

Deck

K
10-4x11

Dining
11x13-4

Garage
19-8x23-4

Dn

P

Living
18x12-8

Up

Vaulted Ceiling

30'-2"

No. 90356

MAIN FLOOR PLAN

One-Level Living is a Breeze

No. 10656

Zoned for privacy and convenience, this contemporary ranch is a perfect home for people who like to entertain. The central foyer divides quiet and active areas. Sound deadening closets and a full bath with double vanities keep the noise to a minimum in the bedroom wing. The deck off the master suite is a nice, private retreat for sunbathing or stargazing. Look at the recessed ceilings and bay windows in the dining room off the foyer. What a beautiful room for a candlelit dinner. Living areas at the rear of the house surround a brick patio so guests can enjoy the outdoors in nice weather. And, the open plan of the kitchen, nook, and vaulted Great room keep traffic flowing smoothly, even when there's a crowd.

First floor — 1,899 sq. ft.
Basement — 1,890 sq. ft.
Garage — 530 sq. ft.

Total living area — 1,899 sq. ft.

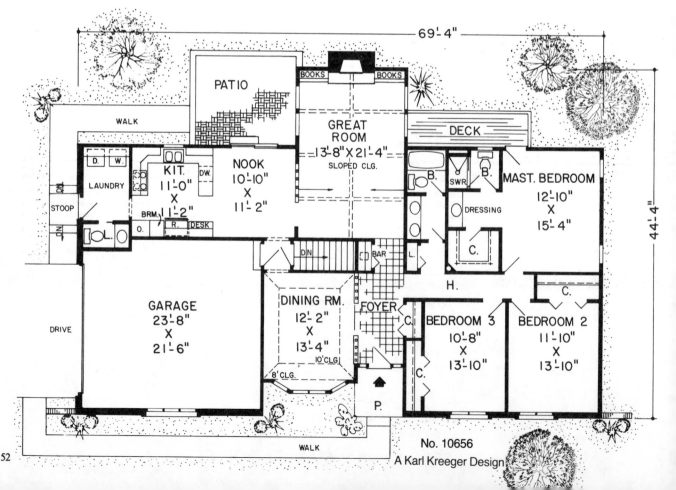

No. 10656
A Karl Kreeger Design

Glass Brings The Outdoors In

No. 9594

Adaptability is the outstanding characteristic of this modern two bedroom home. Imagine a folding partition wall that can enclose part of the expansive dining room to form a guest room or den. When the partitions are not in use, the living room and dining room, separated from the terrace only by sliding glass doors, offer an immense area for entertaining or relaxing. The kitchen is distinguished by an exposed brick wall which encloses the built-in oven.

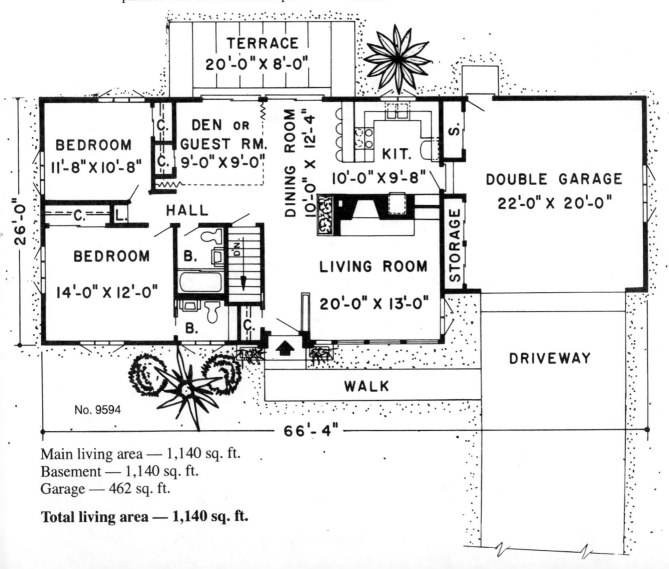

Main living area — 1,140 sq. ft.
Basement — 1,140 sq. ft.
Garage — 462 sq. ft.

Total living area — 1,140 sq. ft.

Great Traffic Pattern Highlights Home

No. 90901

Victorian styling and economical construction techniques make this a doubly charming design. This is a compact charmer brimming with features: a sheltered entry leading to the two-story foyer; an island kitchen with convenient pass-through to the formal dining room; a cozy living room brightened by a bay window; an airy central hall upstairs surrounded by large bedrooms with plenty of closet space. And, look at that lovely master suite with its sitting area in a bay window.

Main floor — 940 sq. ft.

Second floor — 823 sq. ft.

Unfinished basement — 940 sq. ft.

Garage — 440 sq. ft.

Width — 54'-0"

Depth — 33'-0".

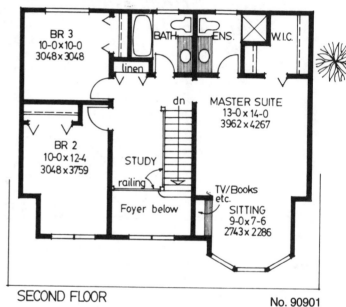

BR 3
10-0 x 10-0
3048 x 3048

BATH

ENS.

W.I.C.

linen

dn

MASTER SUITE
13-0 x 14-0
3962 x 4267

BR 2
10-0 x 12-4
3048 x 3759

STUDY

railing

Foyer below

TV/Books etc.

SITTING
9-0 x 7-6
2743 x 2286

SECOND FLOOR

No. 90901

Total living area — 1,763 sq. ft.

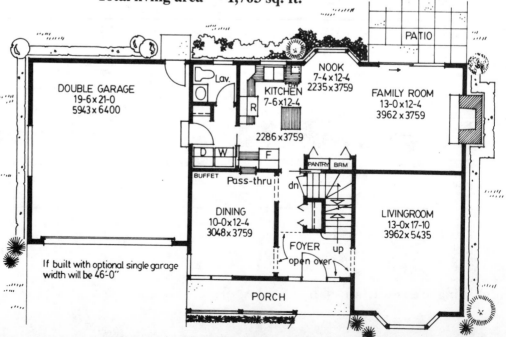

PATIO

DOUBLE GARAGE
19-6 x 21-0
5943 x 6400

Lav.

NOOK
7-4 x 12-4
2235 x 3759

KITCHEN
7-6 x 12-4
2286 x 3759

FAMILY ROOM
13-0 x 12-4
3962 x 3759

R

D W

F

BUFFET

Pass-thru

PANTRY

BRM

dn

DINING
10-0 x 12-4
3048 x 3759

FOYER
open over

up

LIVINGROOM
13-0 x 17-10
3962 x 5435

If built with optional single garage width will be 46'-0"

PORCH

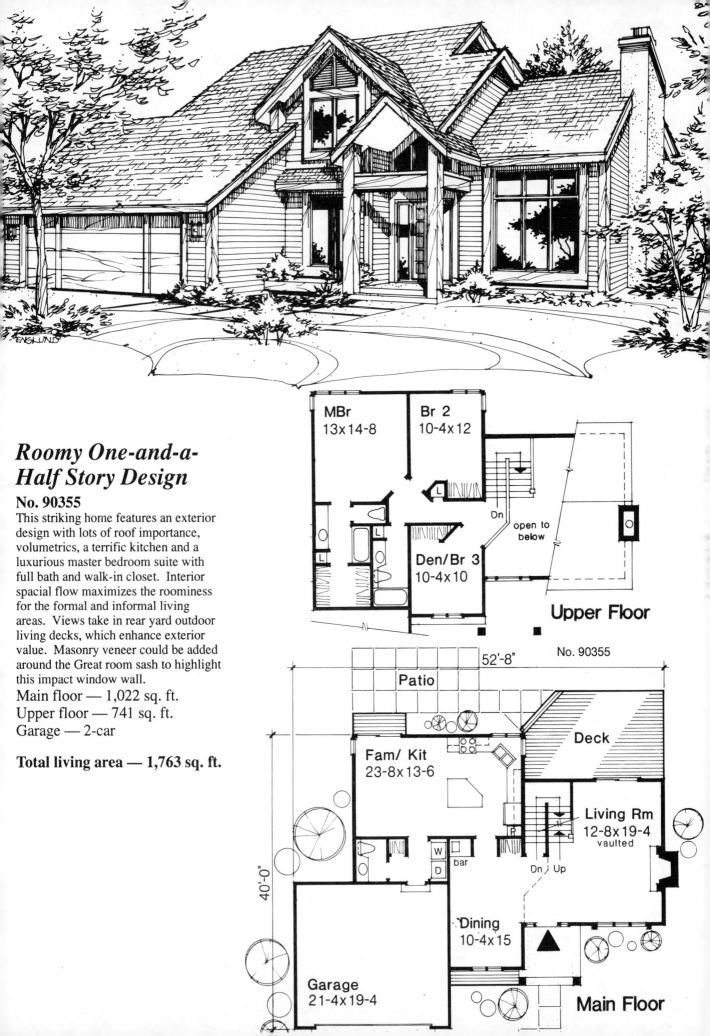

Roomy One-and-a-Half Story Design

No. 90355

This striking home features an exterior design with lots of roof importance, volumetrics, a terrific kitchen and a luxurious master bedroom suite with full bath and walk-in closet. Interior spacial flow maximizes the roominess for the formal and informal living areas. Views take in rear yard outdoor living decks, which enhance exterior value. Masonry veneer could be added around the Great room sash to highlight this impact window wall.

Main floor — 1,022 sq. ft.
Upper floor — 741 sq. ft.
Garage — 2-car

Total living area — 1,763 sq. ft.

Upper Floor

MBr
13x14-8

Br 2
10-4x12

Den/Br 3
10-4x10

Dn
open to below

Main Floor

No. 90355

52'-8"
40'-0"

Patio

Deck

Fam/ Kit
23-8x13-6

Living Rm
12-8x19-4
vaulted

W D
bar
Dn Up

Dining
10-4x15

Garage
21-4x19-4

Greek Revival

No. 99610

The large front entrance porch with its pediment and columns, although classical in style, presents a farmhouse quality. The 11'-0" ceiling height for the foyer and 25 foot long living room, the focal point of which is a stunning, brick-faced, heat-circulating fireplace flanked by cabinetry and shelves, give a spacious feeling throughout. The formal dining room with a bayed window, connects to the living room and kitchen and overlooks a large rear terrace. The private bedroom wing, separately zoned from the main active living spaces, contains three bedrooms and two baths. One bath with two basins and a whirlpool tub serves the master bedroom while the other is shared by the other two bedrooms. The master bath has sliding glass doors which connect to a private terrace.

Main living area — 1,460 sq. ft.
Lndry/mudroom — 68 sq. ft.
Garage & Storage — 494 sq. ft.
Basement — 1,367 sq. ft.

Total living area — 1,460 sq. ft.

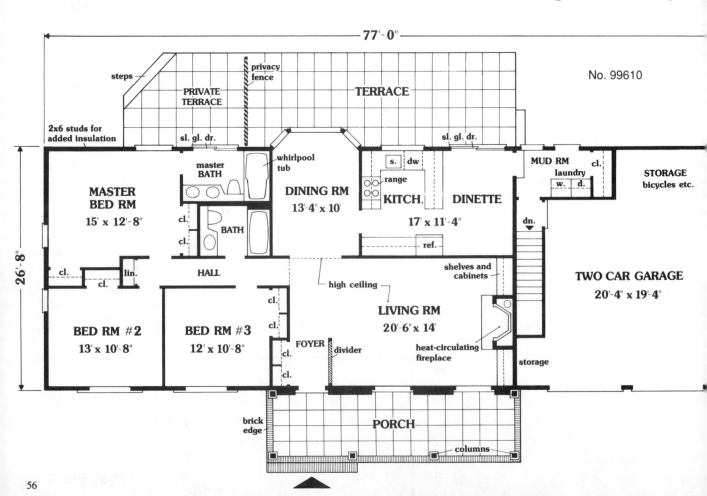

Formal Balance

No. 90689

Here's a magnificent example of classical design with a contemporary twist. The graceful columns that adorn the facade of this one-level beauty also separate interior spaces without walls. Combined with the half-round windows in the living room, they create an open, elegant feeling throughout formal areas. A bow window in the dining room overlooking the deck echoes the classic image. Kitchen and dinette share the open atmosphere, flowing together into a spacious unit that opens to the rear deck through sliding glass doors. The master suite enjoys a private corner of the deck, complete with hot-tub, double-vanitied bath, and ample closets. Two front-facing bedrooms across the hall share another full bath.

Main living area — 1,374 sq. ft.
Mudroom-laundry — 102 sq. ft.
Basement — 1,361 sq. ft.
Garage — 548 sq. ft.

Total living area — 1,476 sq. ft.

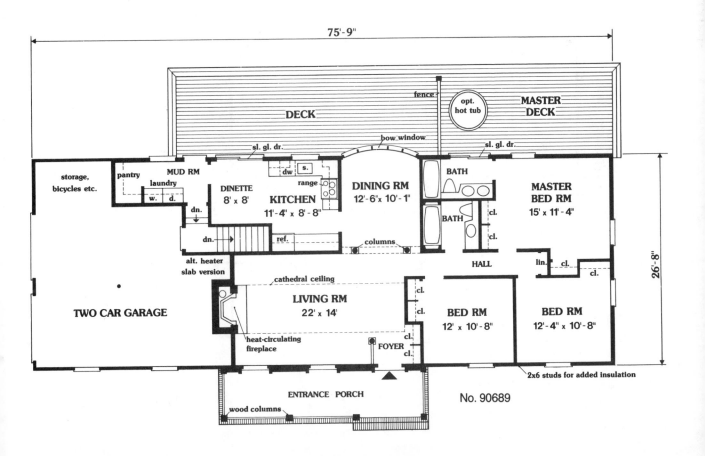

Cozy Traditional With Style

No. 99208

This charming one-story traditional home greets visitors with a covered porch. A galley-style kitchen shares a snack bar with the spacious gathering room where a fireplace is the focal point. An ample master suite includes a luxury bath with a whirlpool tub and separate dressing room. Two additional bedrooms, one that could double as a study, are located at the front of the home.

Basement — 1,830 sq. ft.
Garage — 2-car

Total living area — 1,830 sq. ft.

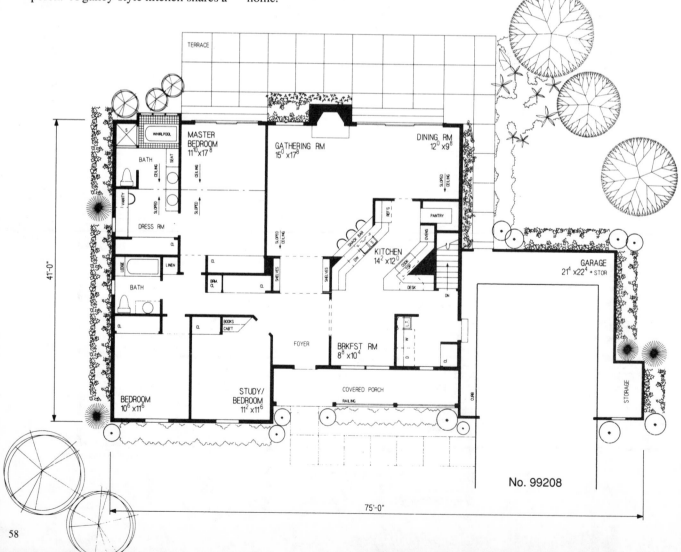

No. 99208

Open Living Area Highlights Well-Zoned Plan

No. 10523

A feeling of spaciousness is created by the centrally located living and dining areas which both have a view of the hearth fireplace. The galley-style kitchen features a pantry, a bump-out window over the sink, and easy access to the combined laundry/utility room. The breakfast nook, which overlooks the deck, is flooded with light from the uniquely arranged windows. The three bedrooms and two baths are on the other side of the core of activity rooms. The master bedroom has a private bath plus a double vanity and a walk-in closet in the dressing area.

Main living area — 1,737 sq. ft.
Basement — 1,737 sq. ft.
Garage — 584 sq. ft.

Total living area — 1,737 sq. ft.

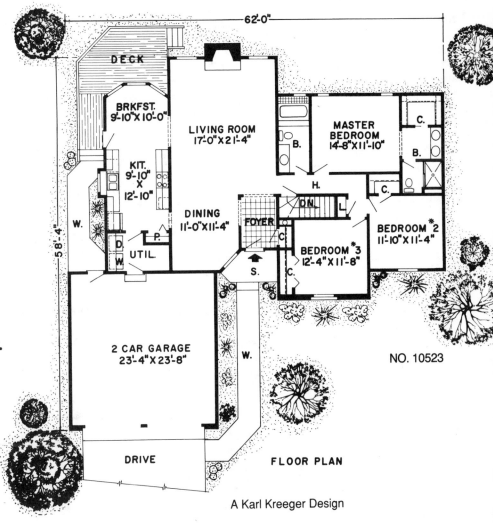

NO. 10523

FLOOR PLAN

A Karl Kreeger Design

Western Approach to the Ranch House

No. 90007

Here is a house in authentic ranch style with long loggia, posts and braces, hand-split shake roof, and cross-buck doors. Two wings sprawl at an angle on either side of a Texas-sized hexagonal living room. Directly across from the double-door entrance, a sunken living room is two steps lower and enhanced by two solid walls (one pierced by a fireplace), two ten-foot walls of almost solid glass (with sliding glass doors), and two walls opened wide as entrances from foyer and to dining room. For outdoor living and dining, a porch surrounds the room on three sides.

Main living area — 1,830 sq. ft.
Garage — 2-car

Total living area — 1,830 sq. ft.

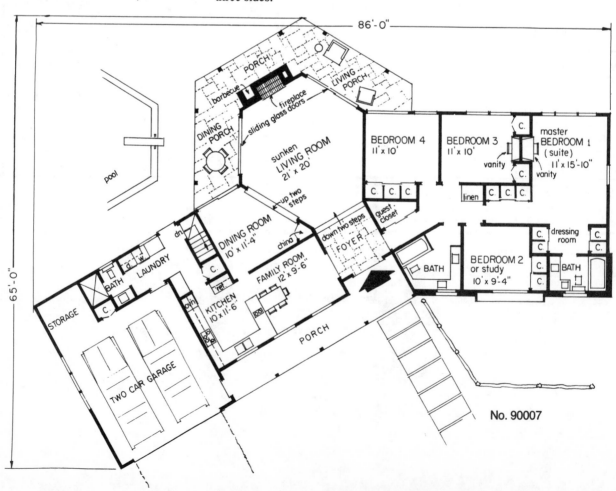

Rustic Vacation House

No. 90004

This compact three-bedroom cabin, designed for vacations and late retirement, would suit many areas. The stone and wood exterior requires little maintenance. Two porches and an outdoor balcony make the most of entertaining, relaxing, or just enjoying a sunset. From the foyer you can see the spiral stairway which leads to a balcony and an upstairs bedroom or studio. A wood fire always seems to make a house warmer and cozier, and this design includes a massive stone fireplace in the living room. The living room also has a pair of floor-to-ceiling windows at the gable end and sliding glass doors to a rear porch. There is a pantry adjoining the eat-in kitchen which has a small bay window over the sink. Off the foyer is a powder room. The design also includes two bedrooms and a bath on the first floor.

First floor — 1,020 sq. ft.
Second floor — 265 sq. ft.

Total living area — 1,285 sq. ft.

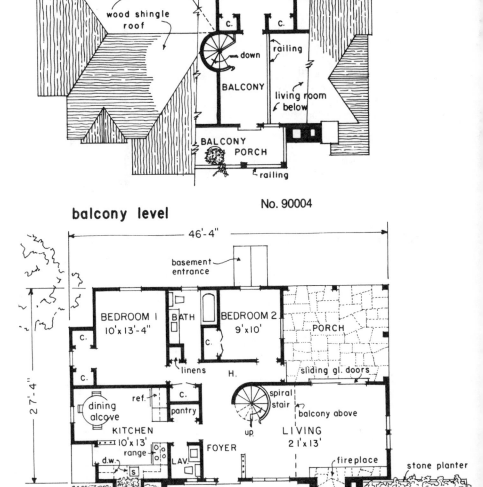

balcony level

No. 90004

first floor

Functional Home With Distinct Features

No. 91646

This deceptively simple plan describes a functional home with features usually found only in much larger dwellings. Although at 50'x50', it will fit on almost any lot. There are three bedrooms and a den. The master bedroom with double doors, his and her sinks and a spacious walk-in closet give a taste of luxury. The modern kitchen enjoys easy access to all parts of the home and boasts a utility room of generous size.

Main living area — 1,422 sq. ft.

Total living area — 1,422 sq. ft.

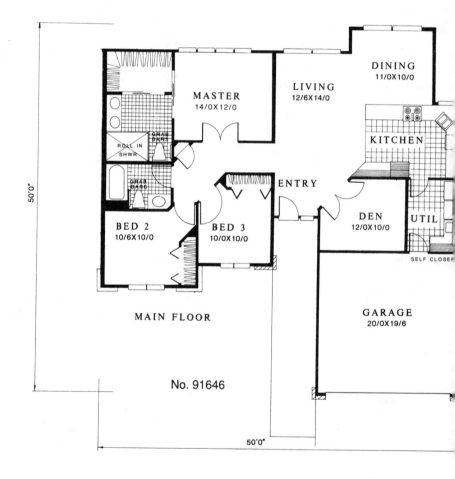

MASTER
14/0X12/0

LIVING
12/6X14/0

DINING
11/0X10/0

GRAB BARS

ROLL IN SHWR

GRAB BARS

KITCHEN

ENTRY

DEN
12/0X10/0

UTIL

SELF CLOSER

BED 2
10/6X10/0

BED 3
10/0X10/0

50'0"

MAIN FLOOR

GARAGE
20/0X19/6

No. 91646

50'0"

62

Exciting Ceilings

No. 20191

The uniquely shaped foyer leads into an elegant living room which includes a brick hearth fireplace and an eleven and a half foot ceiling. The dining room which flows into the kitchen has a decorative ceiling and has access to a deck. One side of the house contains the two additional bedrooms which share a bathroom. The opposite side of the house contains a very private master bedroom suite with a decorative ceiling and huge walk-in closet. The house also includes a two-car garage.

Main living area — 1,606 sq. ft.
Basement — 1,575 sq. ft.
Garage — 545 sq. ft.

Total living area — 1,606 sq. ft.

No. 20191

60'-0"

40'-0"

A Karl Kreeger Design

Deck

Br 3
11 x 11-8

MBr 1
13-8 x 13
decor. ceiling

Kitchen
11 x 13-4

Dining Rm
12 x 13-4
decor. ceiling

W | D   pan.

DN

lin.

Br 2
11-4 x 11-8

Garage
21-4 x 21-8

Living Rm
21 x 15-4
11'-6" ceiling ht.

Foyer

Varied Roof Heights Create Interesting Lines

No. 90601

This rambling one-story Colonial farmhouse packs a lot of living space into its compact plan. The covered porch, enriched by arches, columns and Colonial details, is the focal point of the facade. Inside, the house is zoned for convenience. Formal living and dining rooms occupy the front of the house. To the rear are the family room, island kitchen, and dinette. The family room features a heat-circulating fireplace, visible from the entrance foyer, and sliding glass doors to the large rear patio. Three bedrooms and two baths are away from the action in a private wing.

Main living area — 1,536 sq. ft.
Garage 2-car
(Optional slab construction available)

Total living area — 1,536 sq. ft.

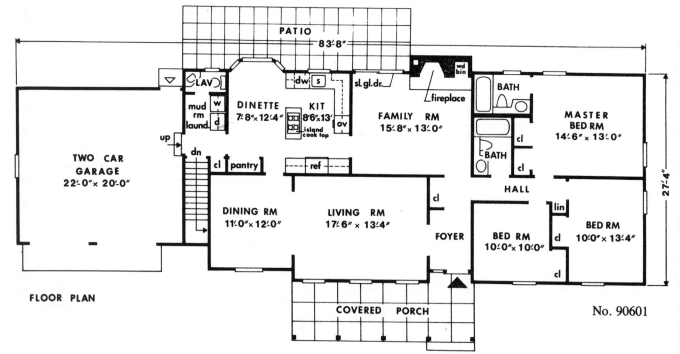

FLOOR PLAN

No. 90601

Bays Add Beauty and Living Space

No. 90607

The welcoming warmth that most Traditional houses seem to exude is especially evident in this center hall, four-bedroom residence. Just off the two-story foyer, the formal living room features a heat-circulating fireplace. Ionic columns and a semi-circular window wall give the dining room a classic grace. The U-shaped kitchen opens to the fireplaced family room. Off the foyer, there are two bedrooms and two baths. Two bedrooms upstairs share a bath.

First floor — 1,515 sq. ft.
Second floor — 530 sq. ft.
Garage — 2-car

Total living area — 2,045 sq. ft.

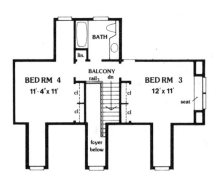

SECOND FLOOR PLAN

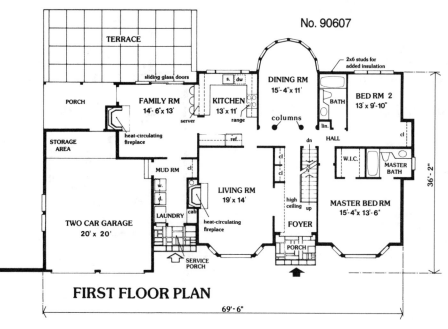

FIRST FLOOR PLAN

Private Places

No. 90563

The central entry does more than just welcome guests to this spacious, one-level home; it separates active and quiet areas for privacy. In the bedroom wing, you'll find three bedrooms and two full baths. The master suite is a special treat, with its huge, walk-in closet, double vanities, separate toilet area, and jacuzzi tub. The living and dining rooms open to the entry for a wide-open feeling accentuated by towering windows and high ceilings. And, overlooking the backyard, the kitchen of your dreams features a cooktop island, a bayed breakfast nook, and an adjoining family room complete with a cozy fireplace.

Main living area — 1,990 sq. ft.
Garage — 2-car

Total living area — 1,990 sq. ft.

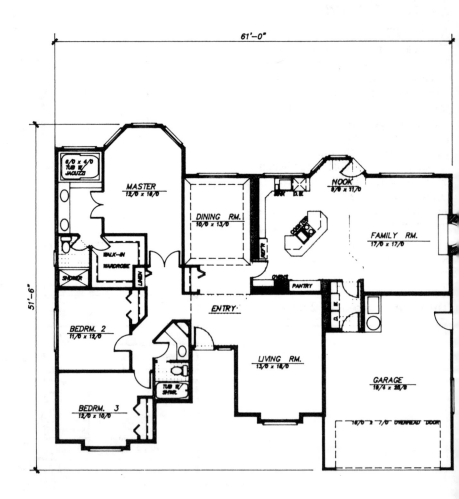

No. 90563

Traditional

No. 91442

This traditional home presents the look and feel of grandeur in only 1,642 square feet. The master suite features a walk-in closet and private patio. Separate living and family room provide extra space for active people. The garage is accessible from both the front and the right. The covered entry with trella provides an excellent area for planting. The residence measures 55' in width and 56' in depth.

Main floor — 1,642 sq. ft.

Garage — 2-car

Total living area— 1,642 sq. ft.

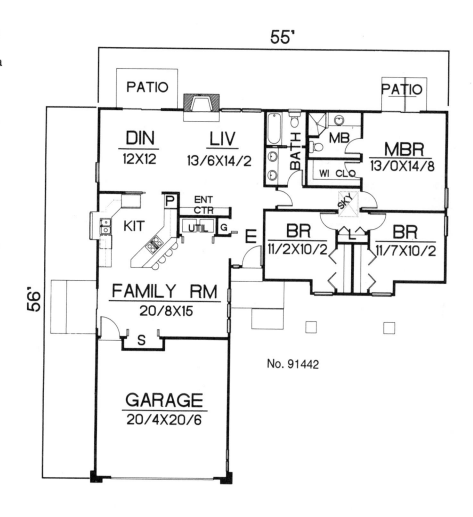

55'

56'

PATIO

PATIO

DIN
12X12

LIV
13/6X14/2

BATH

MB

MBR
13/0X14/8

WI CLO

P

ENT
CTR

KIT

UTIL

G

E

SKY

BR
11/2X10/2

BR
11/7X10/2

FAMILY RM
20/8X15

S

GARAGE
20/4X20/6

No. 91442

Living Room Features Vaulted Ceiling

No. 90353

This 3-bedroom home will appeal to today's style-sensitive buyer. The flowing roof lines and volumes of its design make the house seem larger than its real size. The living room features a vaulted ceiling and the dining room, with clerestory above, opens onto a backyard patio. The master bedroom has a full bath and walk-in closet. Two more bedrooms and another bath are located on the upper floor. The design features basement construction detailing and exterior wall construction.

Main floor — 846 sq. ft.
Upper floor — 400 sq. ft.
Garage — 2-car

Total living area — 1,246 sq. ft.

No. 90353

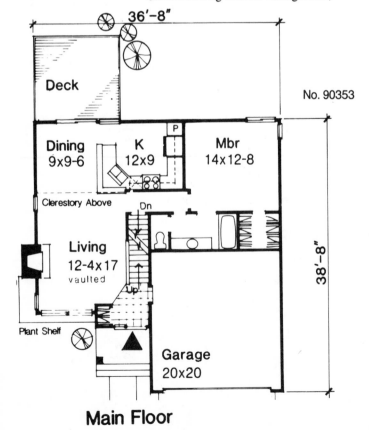

Main Floor

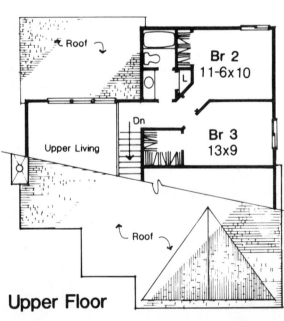

Upper Floor

Open Plan Features Great Room and Exterior Options

No. 90328

With a skylight and a vaulted ceiling, the gGreat room will welcome family and guests alike. This inviting room also includes a fireplace, sliding door access to the deck and a wetbar. The roomy eat-in kitchen features an

efficient U-shaped work area and lots of windows in the dining area. The three bedrooms and two full baths incorporate unusual angled entries so as to make the most of every foot of floor space. The master bedroom combines its bath and dressing area. The third bedroom would make a cozy den or a handy room for guests.

Main living area — 1,400 sq. ft.
Basement — 1,350 sq. ft.
Garage — 374 sq. ft.

Total living area — 1,400 sq. ft.

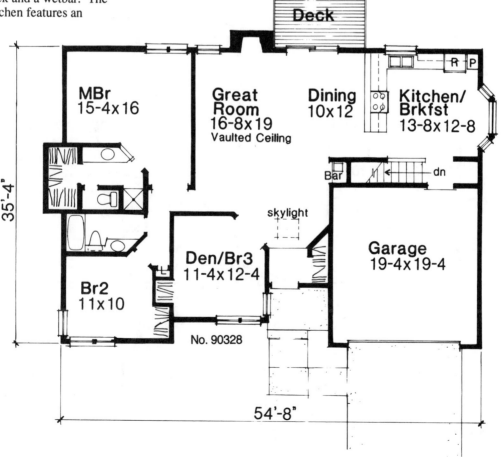

Deck

MBr
15-4x16

Great Room
16-8x19
Vaulted Ceiling

Dining
10x12

Kitchen/
Brkfst
13-8x12-8

Bar

dn

skylight

Den/Br3
11-4x12-4

Garage
19-4x19-4

Br2
11x10

No. 90328

35'-4"

54'-8"

Contemporary Exterior

No. 90327

A spacious feeling is created by the ingenious arrangement of the living areas of this comfortable home. The inviting living room offers a cozy fireplace, a front corner full of windows, a vaulted ceiling and an open staircase. The clerestory windows further accent the open design of the dining room and kitchen. The U-shaped kitchen welcomes cook and tasters alike with its open preparation areas. Secluded from the rest of the main floor and the other two bedrooms, the master bedroom features a walk-in closet and a large, compartmented bath which may also serve as a guest bathroom. Two additional bedrooms and a full bath comprise the upper floor.

Main floor — 846 sq. ft.
Upper floor — 400 sq. ft.
Basement — 846 sq. ft.
Garage — 400 sq. ft.

Total living area — 1,246 sq. ft.

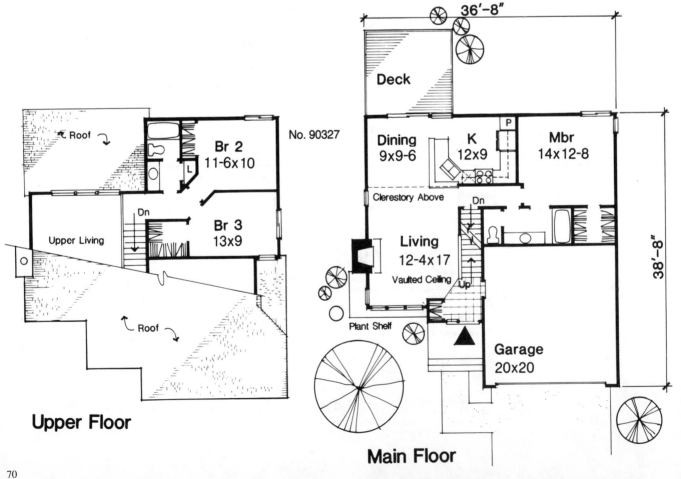

Upper Floor

Main Floor

Appeal Everyone Wants

No. 92016

This house will surely turn heads with its repeating front gables, shuttered windows, and wrap-around front porch. Just pass through the entry and be treated to a long view to the corner glass and fireplace conversation area in the Great room. The large family/kitchen opens to a screened porch and private side deck. The rear located open stair offers a privacy you can't get with entry stair cases. Upstairs you will find a large master bedroom with private bath, a second bath, two additional bedrooms, and laundry facilities.

First floor — 760 sq. ft.
Second floor — 728 sq. ft.
Basement — 768 sq. ft.
Garage — 407 sq. ft.

Total living area — 1,488 sq. ft.

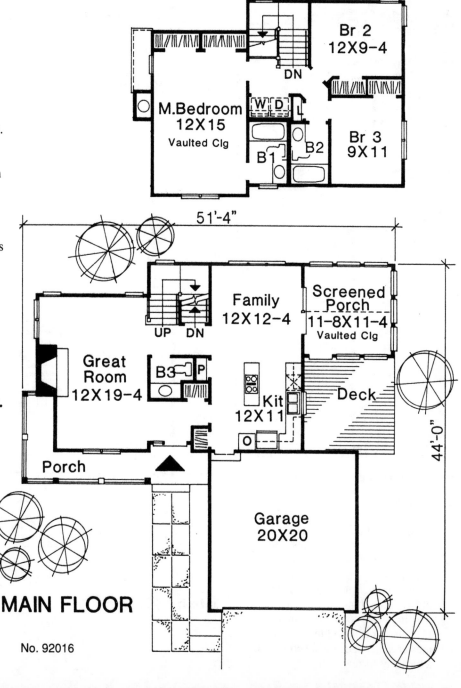

MAIN FLOOR

No. 92016

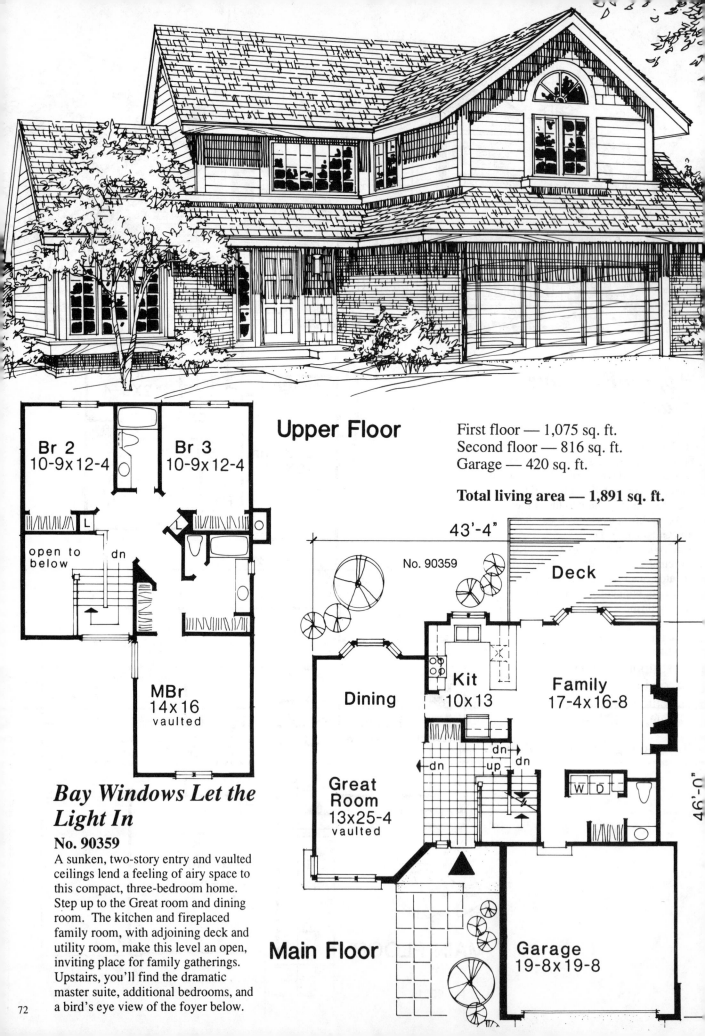

Upper Floor

First floor — 1,075 sq. ft.
Second floor — 816 sq. ft.
Garage — 420 sq. ft.

Total living area — 1,891 sq. ft.

Br 2
10-9 x 12-4

Br 3
10-9 x 12-4

open to below

dn

MBr
14 x 16
vaulted

43'-4"

No. 90359

Deck

Dining

Kit
10 x 13

Family
17-4 x 16-8

dn

dn

up

dn

Great
Room
13 x 25-4
vaulted

W D

46'-0"

Main Floor

Garage
19-8 x 19-8

Bay Windows Let the Light In

No. 90359

A sunken, two-story entry and vaulted ceilings lend a feeling of airy space to this compact, three-bedroom home. Step up to the Great room and dining room. The kitchen and fireplaced family room, with adjoining deck and utility room, make this level an open, inviting place for family gatherings. Upstairs, you'll find the dramatic master suite, additional bedrooms, and a bird's eye view of the foyer below.

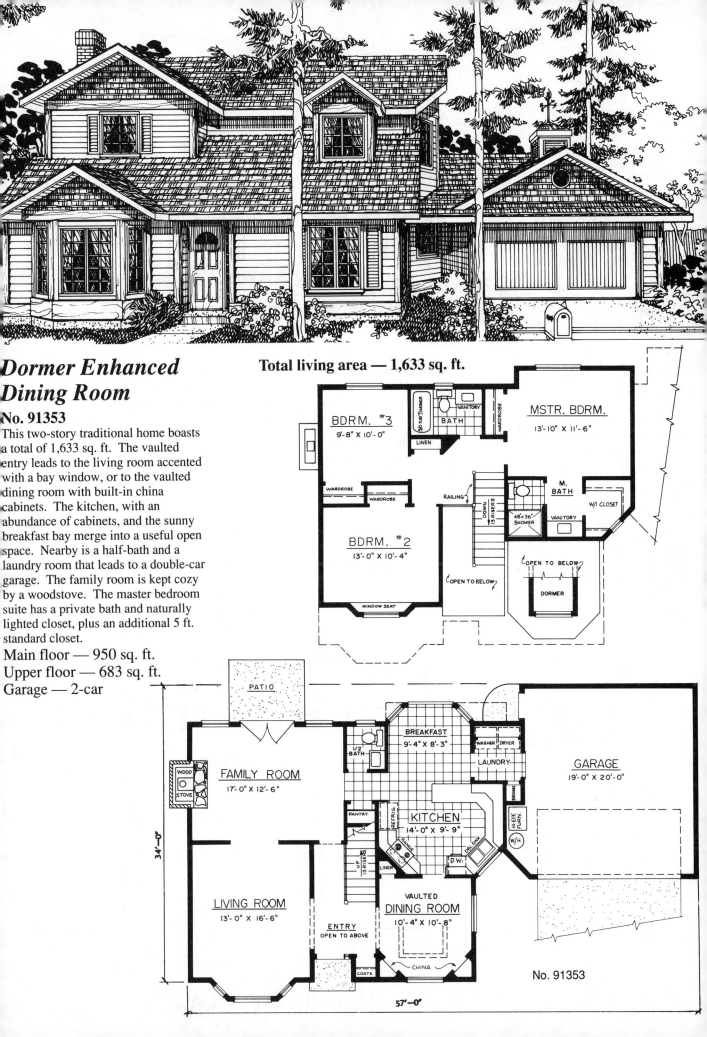

Dormer Enhanced Dining Room

No. 91353

This two-story traditional home boasts a total of 1,633 sq. ft. The vaulted entry leads to the living room accented with a bay window, or to the vaulted dining room with built-in china cabinets. The kitchen, with an abundance of cabinets, and the sunny breakfast bay merge into a useful open space. Nearby is a half-bath and a laundry room that leads to a double-car garage. The family room is kept cozy by a woodstove. The master bedroom suite has a private bath and naturally lighted closet, plus an additional 5 ft. standard closet.

Main floor — 950 sq. ft.
Upper floor — 683 sq. ft.
Garage — 2-car

Total living area — 1,633 sq. ft.

BDRM. #3
9'-8" X 10'-0"

BATH

MSTR. BDRM.
13'-10" X 11'-6"

LINEN

WARDROBE

WARDROBE

RAILING

DOWN 13 RISERS

48"x36" SHOWER

M. BATH

W/I CLOSET

VANITORY

BDRM. #2
13'-0" X 10'-4"

OPEN TO BELOW

OPEN TO BELOW

DORMER

WINDOW SEAT

PATIO

FAMILY ROOM
17'-0" X 12'-6"

WOOD STOVE

1/2 BATH

BREAKFAST
9'-4" X 8'-3"

WASHER DRYER

LAUNDRY

GARAGE
19'-0" X 20'-0"

PANTRY

REFRIG.

KITCHEN
14'-0" X 9'-9"

Hi-EFF. FURN.

W/H

UP 13 RISERS

LINEN

RANGE

D.W.

DBL. SINK

LIVING ROOM
13'-0" X 16'-6"

VAULTED DINING ROOM
10'-4" X 10'-8"

ENTRY
OPEN TO ABOVE

CHINA

COATS

No. 91353

34'-0"

57'-0"

Secluded Vacation Retreat

No. 91704

The interior space design of this plan makes it quite suitable as a vacation home. A bedroom wing extends on either side of the high vaulted-living area, and offers extensive privacy. The two bedrooms on the main level are large, with 10-foot closets, and each has its own personal bath, double vanity and secluded patio, which is protected by the extended walls of the main living area. The living room is generous, with a large masonry fireplace and a circular stairway

dominating the center of the house. One wall features windows along its full cathedral height. The kitchen has lots of counter space and cupboards, including a sink and chopping block island. The circular stairway leads to a loft room above. This could be a library, a guest bedroom, or a third

bedroom. From this room, windowed doors open to a deck that is also the roof for the carport below.

First floor — 1,448 sq. ft.
Loft plan — 389 sq. ft.
Carport — 312 sq. ft.

Total living area — 1,837 sq. ft.

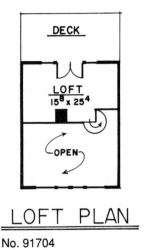

LOFT PLAN

No. 91704

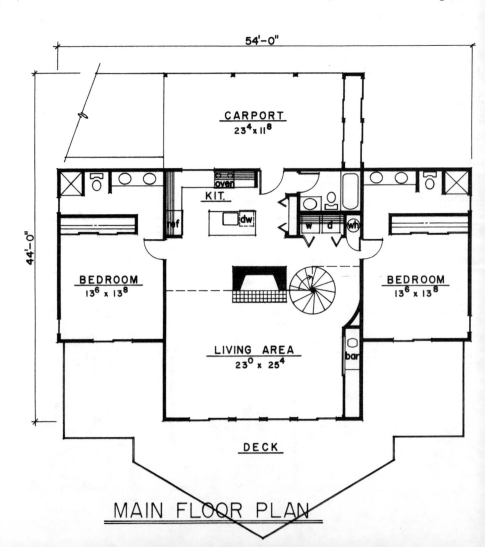

MAIN FLOOR PLAN

A-Frame for Year-Round Living

No. 90930

If you have a hillside lot, this open design may be just what you've been looking for. With three bedrooms, it's a perfect plan for your growing family. The roomy foyer opens to a hallway that leads to the kitchen, bedrooms, and a dramatic, vaulted living room with a massive fireplace. A wrap-around sundeck gives you lots of outdoor living space. And, upstairs, there's a special retreat — a luxurious master suite complete with its own private deck.

Main floor — 1,238 sq. ft.
Loft — 464 sq. ft.
Basement — 1,175 sq. ft.
Width — 34 ft.
Depth — 56 ft.

Total living area — 1,702 sq. ft.

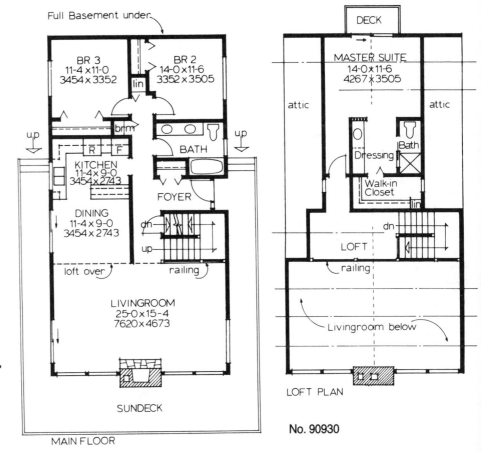

Stately Home Features Formal Courtyard

No. 90014

Gracing the entrance of this elegant home is formal courtyard complete with reflecting pool. The grand foyer leads to the large living room which features a fireplace, window seats and an archway opening onto the dining room. The side terrace is easily reached through the dining room's French doors. The conveniently organized kitchen is located between the dining room and the family room, which is expanded by its French door entrances to both the front courtyard and the more informal porch. The three bedrooms located on the second floor are arranged to make the most efficient use of space.

First floor — 943 sq. ft.
Second floor — 772 sq. ft.

Total living area — 1,715 sq. ft.

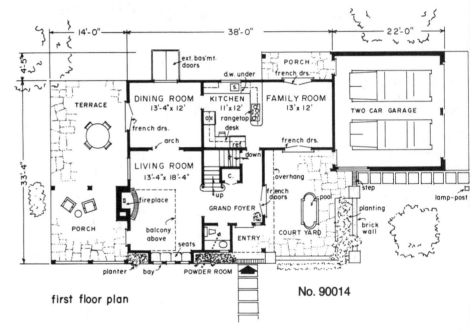

first floor plan   No. 90014

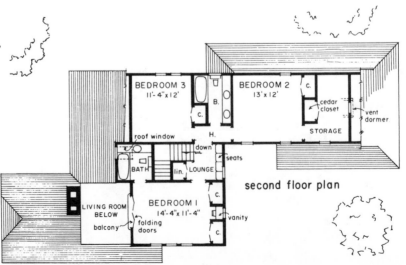

second floor plan

Design Portrays Expensive Taste

No. 90040

Inside the front entrance and beyond the foyer, a square reception hall divides traffic to either living or service area. Located here is a powder room for easy guest use. To the left, the 20 x 13 living room — with its 8-foot wide bank of front windows, log burning fireplace and French doors to the connecting porch — provides adequate, comfortable space for entertaining. Its use will continue to be appreciated over years of day-to-day living. The curved staircase to the second floor leads to the sleeping level. To the right is a large storage area. A space to the rear could be finished as a den or office which still would leave plenty of storage. Two baths offer more than adequate service for the three bedrooms. A round master bath is located in the turret.

First floor — 1,069 sq. ft.
Second floor — 948 sq. ft.
Garage — 546 sq. ft.
Porch — 120 sq. ft.
Screened Porch — 292 sq. ft.

Total living area — 2,017 sq. ft.

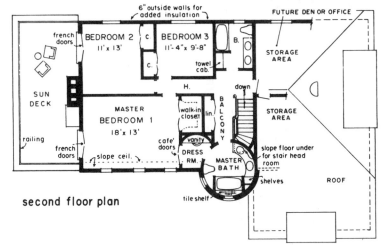

second floor plan

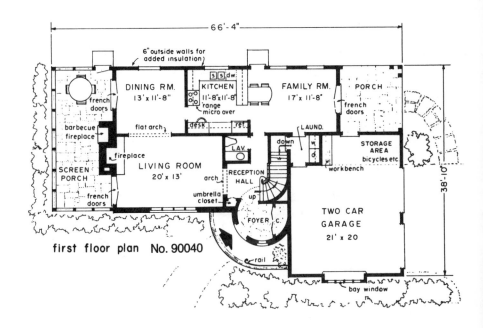

first floor plan   No. 90040

Outdoor-Lovers' Delight

No. 90248

If outdoor entertaining is your pleasure, this is the perfect house. Rain or shine, the covered porch off the dining room provides shelter, while the rear terrace lets you have fun in the sun. And, every room enjoys an outdoor atmosphere, thanks to sliding glass doors and oversized windows. The well-appointed kitchen, centrally located just steps away from formal dinners, family suppers in the breakfast nook, or h'ors doeuvres in the soaring gathering room, is a cook's dream. Three bedrooms, tucked down a hall off the foyer, include the spacious master suite with its own private terrace access and full bath with step-in shower.

Main living area — 1,729 sq. ft.
Garage — 2-car

Total living area — 1,729 sq. ft.

OPTIONAL NON-BASEMENT

No. 90248

68'-0"

48'-8"

TERRACE

GATHERING RM.
16⁰ x 20⁴

SLOPED CEILING

DINING RM.
12⁰ x 10⁰

COVERED DINING PORCH

WALK-IN CLOSET

MASTER BEDROOM
11⁰ x 15⁴

BATH

TUB

BATH

KITCHEN
12⁰ x 11⁰

PANTRY

MUD RM.

STORAGE
13⁰ x 9⁸

CL

LINEN

CL

FOYER

SNACK BAR

CURB

BEDROOM
11⁰ x 12⁸

COVERED PORCH

STUDY/ BEDROOM
10⁰ x 11⁰

BREAKFAST RM.
14⁴ x 8⁰ + BAY

GARAGE
21⁴ x 21⁴

78

SECOND FLOOR PLAN

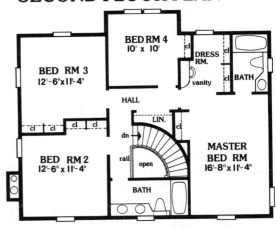

BED RM 4
10' x 10'

DRESS RM.

BATH

BED RM 3
12'-6" x 11'-4"

vanity

HALL

cl

LIN.

cl

BED RM 2
12'-6" x 11'-4"

dn

rail

open

MASTER BED RM
16'-8" x 11'-4"

BATH

Built-In Entertainment Center for Family Fun

No. 90615

Up-to-date features bring this center hall Colonial into the 20th century. The focus of the Early American living room is a heat-circulating fireplace, framed by decorative pilasters that support dropped beams. Both dining areas open to the rear terrace through sliding glass doors. The convenient mudroom provides access to the two-car garage. Four bedrooms and two baths, including the spacious master suite, occupy the second floor.

First floor — 1,037 sq. ft.
Second floor — 936 sq. ft.
Garage — 441 sq. ft.
(optional slab construction available)
Total living area — 1,973 sq. ft.

FIRST FLOOR PLAN

No. 90615

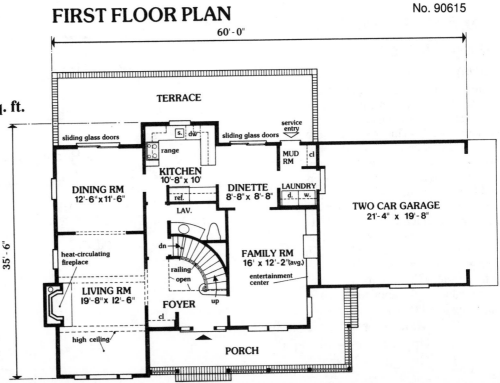

60'-0"

35'-6"

TERRACE

sliding glass doors

s. dw

range

sliding glass doors

service entry

MUD RM

cl

DINING RM
12'-6" x 11'-6"

KITCHEN
10'-8" x 10'

ref.

DINETTE
8'-8" x 8'-8"

LAUNDRY

d. w.

TWO CAR GARAGE
21'-4" x 19'-8"

heat-circulating fireplace

LAV.

dn

railing

open

FAMILY RM
16' x 12'-2" (avg.)

entertainment center

LIVING RM
19'-8" x 12'-6"

FOYER

up

cl

high ceiling

PORCH

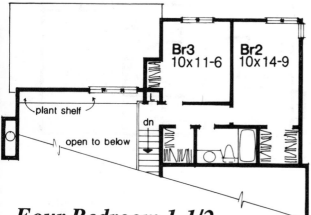

Br3
10x11-6

Br2
10x14-9

plant shelf

dn

open to below

Upper Floor

Total living area — 1,531 sq. ft.

Four Bedroom 1-1/2 Story Design

No. 90358

Many of todays single family markets are looking for a flexible plan that grows and adapts to their family's changing needs. This is such a house with its master bedroom and den/4th bedroom down, double bedrooms up, stacked baths and well-working open and flowing living areas. The exterior impact is of hi-style, hi-value; the interior is highlighted by the vaulted living room and thru views to the rear deck and yard. This house belongs in a neighborhood where the custom exterior look will make for a surprising space-value combination to the move-up young family market.

 Main floor — 1,062 sq. ft.
 Upper floor — 469 sq. ft.
 Garage — 2-car

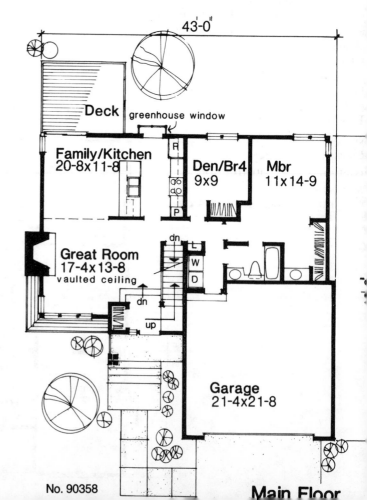

43'-0"

Deck greenhouse window

Family/Kitchen
20-8x11-8

Den/Br4
9x9

Mbr
11x14-9

Great Room
17-4x13-8
vaulted ceiling

dn

up

dn

W
D

Garage
21-4x21-8

Main Floor

No. 90358

Interior and Exterior Unity Distinguishes Plan

No. 90398

Are you a sun worshipper? A rear orientation and a huge, wrap-around deck make this one-level home an outdoor lover's dream. Stepping into the entry, you're afforded a panoramic view of active areas, from the exciting vaulted living room to the angular kitchen overlooking the cheerful breakfast nook. Columns divide the living and dining rooms. Half-walls separate the kitchen and breakfast room. The result is a sunny celebration of open space not often found in a one-level home. Bedrooms feature special window treatments and interesting angles. A full bath serves the two front bedrooms, but the luxurious master suite boasts its own private, skylit bath with double vanities, as well as a generous walk-in closet.

Main living area — 1,630 sq. ft.
Garage — 2-car

Total living area — 1,630 sq. ft.

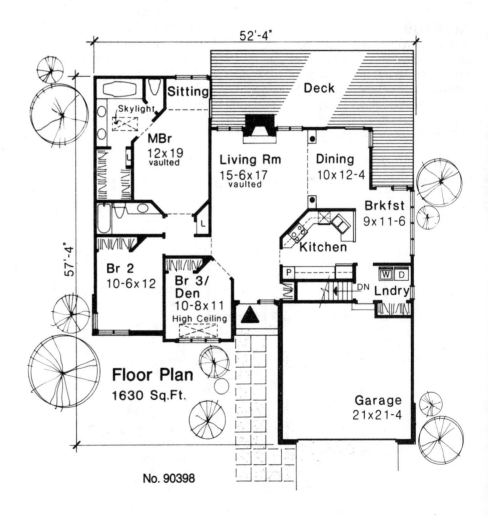

52'-4"

57'-4"

Sitting

Deck

MBr
12x19
vaulted

Skylight

Living Rm
15-6x17
vaulted

Dining
10x12-4

Brkfst
9x11-6

Kitchen

Br 2
10-6x12

Br 3/
Den
10-8x11
High Ceiling

P

W D

DN

Lndry

Floor Plan
1630 Sq.Ft.

Garage
21x21-4

No. 90398

All This On One Level

No. 99619

A gracious feeling welcomes you inside the double entrance doors as you experience natural sky-lighting and flowing space enhanced by a high-sloped ceiling. Featured is the free-standing, heat-circulating fireplace surrounded by stone, to mantle height.

Sliding glass doors connect to a large rear terrace. The adjacent informal space of kitchen, dinette and family room share an openness. The dinette has access to a private dining terrace and the laundry room leading to the garage, basement or side service entrance. The private bedroom wing, accessed via the foyer, contains two large bedrooms, a bath and a master suite off a short corridor. This suite consists of a generously-sized bedroom connecting to a bath with double sinks and window.

Main living area — 1,629 sq. ft.
Lndry/mudroom — 107 sq. ft.
Garage — 424 sq. ft.
Basement — 1,457 sq. ft.

Total living area — 1,629 sq. ft.

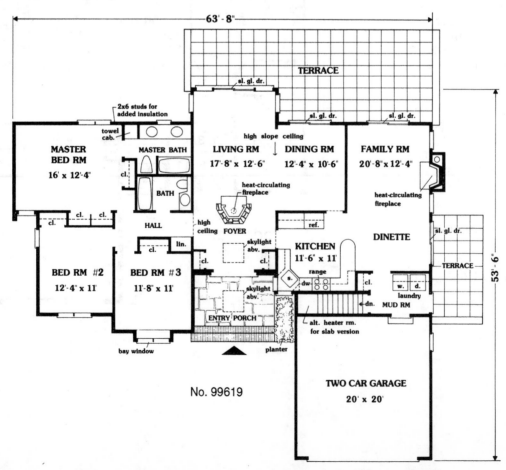

No. 99619

Simple Lines Enhanced by Elegant Window Treatment

No. 34150

Consider this plan if you work at home and would enjoy a homey, well lit office or den. The huge, arched window floods the front room with light. This house offers a lot of other practical details for the two-career family. Compact and efficient use of space means less to clean and organize. Yet the open plan keeps the home from feeling too small and cramped. Other features like plenty of closet space, step-saving laundry facilities, easily-cleaned kitchen, and a window wall in the living room make this a delightful plan.

Main living area — 1,486 sq. ft.
Garage — 462 sq. ft.
Basement — 1,486 sq. ft.

Total living area — 1,486 sq. ft.

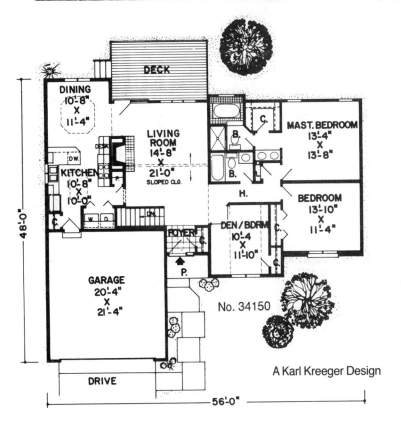

DECK

DINING
10'-8"
X
11'-4"

LIVING ROOM
14'-8"
X
21'-0"
SLOPED CLG.

KITCHEN
10'-8"
X
10'-0"

MAST. BEDROOM
13'-4"
X
13'-8"

BEDROOM
13'-10"
X
11'-4"

DEN / BDRM
10'-4"
X
11'-10"

FOYER

GARAGE
20'-4"
X
21'-4"

48'-0"

56'-0"

DRIVE

No. 34150

A Karl Kreeger Design

Story-book Type Design

No. 90038

Viewed from the front, this story-book home catches the imagination of any passerby. It has interesting construction details such as varied roof lines, nook, porches with posts, full stone veneer gable face, shuttered windows, rustic wood shake shingles, decorative chimney plus board and batten siding, all lend their distinctive touches toward the overall charm. Inside, the front foyer leads to a sunken living room of fair proportions which offers a touch of luxury with its one step down and a stone fireplace. One cannot fail to notice the generous amount of daylight beyond the two sets of double French doors leading to a 19-foot solarium.

First floor — 1,498 sq. ft.
Second floor — 501 sq. ft.

Total living area — 1,999 sq. ft.

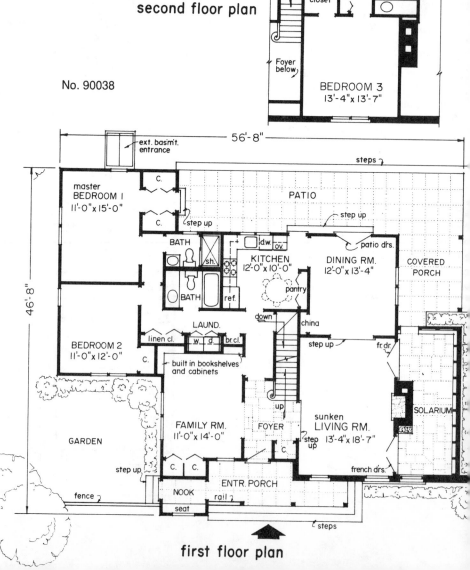

second floor plan

No. 90038

first floor plan

Extra Large Kitchen In Cozy Three Bedroom Home

No. 90134

The center of this three bedroom charmer is the extra large family kitchen. The galley-style food preparation area is located in one corner and separated from the rest of the room by a bar. Its placement near the carport entrance simplifies trips to the grocery store. Another convenience designed into this home is the placement of the laundry between the kitchen and the bedrooms. The three bedrooms are clustered around the full bath and one of the bedrooms features a private lav. In addition to the storage areas built into the living areas, a large outdoor storage closet is located at the back of the carport. This comes with either a basement or slab/crawl combination foundation, please specify when ordering

Main living area — 1,120 sq. ft.

Total living area — 1,120 sq. ft.

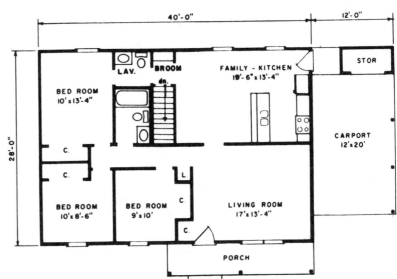

No. 90134 **WITH BASEMENT**

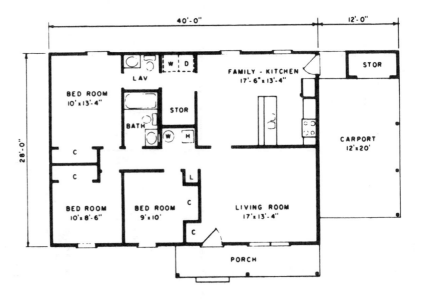

WITHOUT BASEMENT

Compact Plan
Allows For Gracious
Living

No. 90158

A Great room, accessible from the foyer, offers a cathedral ceiling with exposed beams, brick fireplace, and access to the rear patio. The kitchen/breakfast area with center island is accented by the round-top window. The master bedroom has a full bath and walk-in closet. Two

additional bedrooms and bath help make this an ideal plan for any growing family.

Main living area — 1,540 sq. ft.
Basement — 1,540 sq. ft.
Garage — 2-car

Total living area — 1,540 sq. ft.

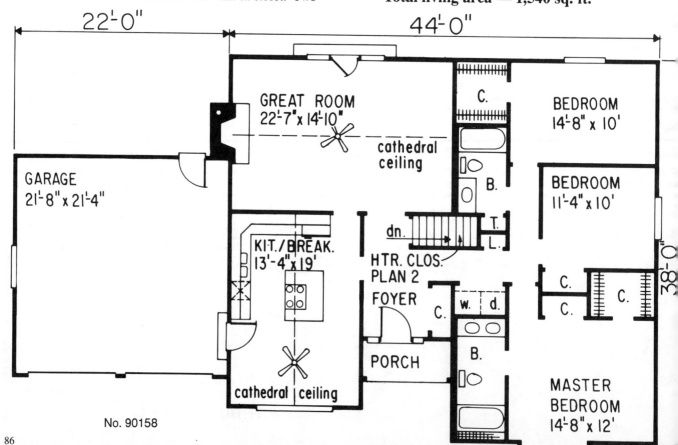

No. 90158

Touch of Nostalgia

No. 92039

The shuttered windows offer a touch of nostalgia to this gabled ranch plan with covered entry. The large living room offers plenty of comfort for those large family gatherings. The large kitchen/dining room has plenty of space for everyone to sit around the table. The plan also features three bedrooms, shared bath, main floor laundry facilities, and utility closet.

Main living area — 1,088 sq. ft.

Total living area — 1,088 sq. ft.
4 or More Occupants

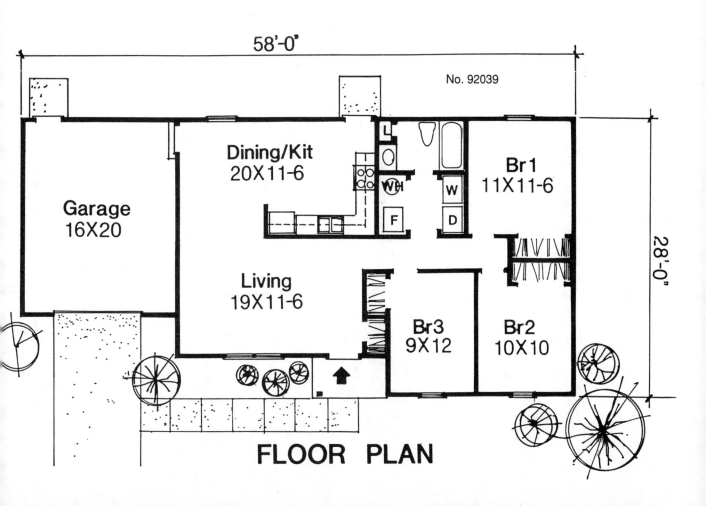

58'-0"

No. 92039

Garage
16X20

Dining/Kit
20X11-6

WH

Br1
11X11-6

W
D
F

Living
19X11-6

Br3
9X12

Br2
10X10

28'-0"

FLOOR PLAN

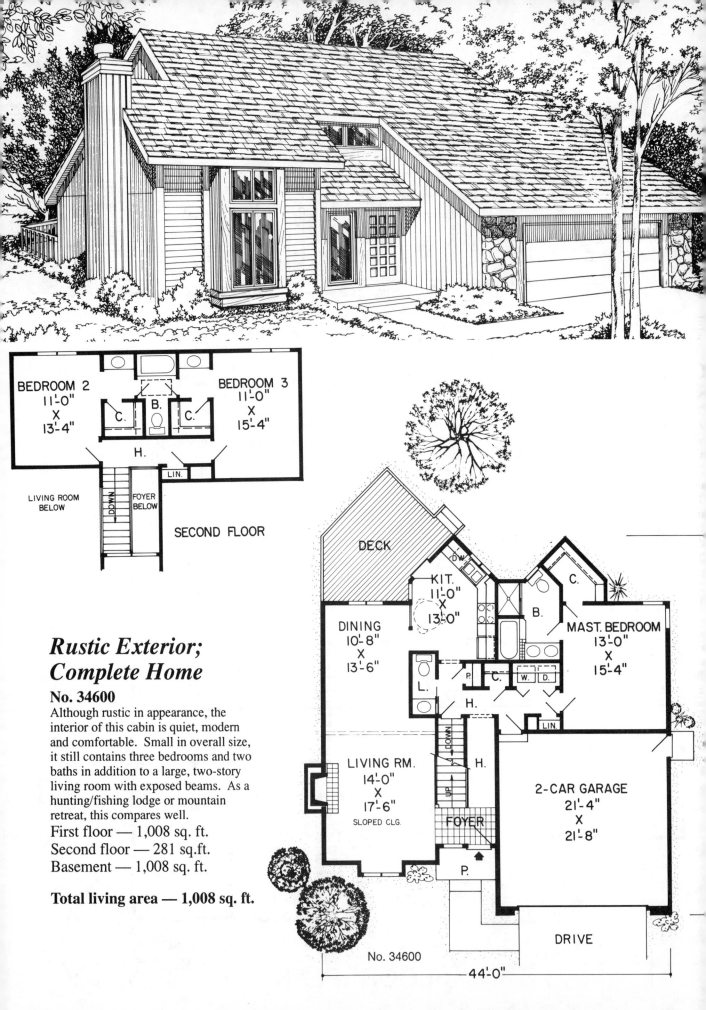

Rustic Exterior; Complete Home

No. 34600

Although rustic in appearance, the interior of this cabin is quiet, modern and comfortable. Small in overall size, it still contains three bedrooms and two baths in addition to a large, two-story living room with exposed beams. As a hunting/fishing lodge or mountain retreat, this compares well.

First floor — 1,008 sq. ft.
Second floor — 281 sq.ft.
Basement — 1,008 sq. ft.

Total living area — 1,008 sq. ft.

BEDROOM 2
11'-0"
X
13'-4"

BEDROOM 3
11'-0"
X
15'-4"

B.

C.

C.

H.

LIVING ROOM BELOW

DOWN

FOYER BELOW

LIN.

SECOND FLOOR

DECK

KIT.
11'-0"
X
13'-0"

DW

C.

B.

DINING
10'-8"
X
13'-6"

MAST. BEDROOM
13'-0"
X
15'-4"

L.

P.

C.

W.

D.

H.

LIN.

LIVING RM.
14'-0"
X
17'-6"

SLOPED CLG.

DOWN

UP

H.

2-CAR GARAGE
21'-4"
X
21'-8"

FOYER

P.

DRIVE

No. 34600

44'-0"

Compact Classic

No. 91413

Designed with economy in mind, this traditional treasure will give you a lot of house for your building dollar. And, its compact shape and attractive Colonial exterior make this home an asset to any neighborhood. The main floor is divided into formal and family areas. Entertain in the living and dining rooms, separated by the L-shaped, open staircase to the second floor. The powder room around the corner means guests don't have to walk upstairs. You'll enjoy the view from the rear of the house, where the kitchen, nook, and family room flow together for a wide-open feeling accentuated by lots of windows and an atrium door to the patio. Upstairs, three bedrooms and two full baths include the spacious master suite.

First floor — 963 sq. ft.
Second floor — 774 sq. ft.
Garage — 2-car

Total living area — 1,737 sq. ft.

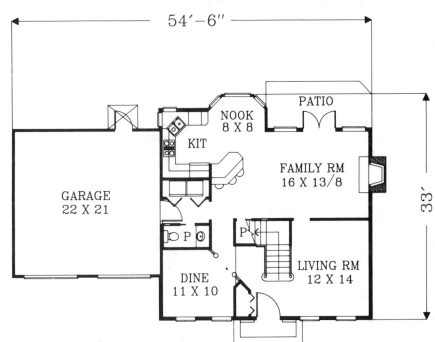

FIRST FLOOR PLAN

No. 91413

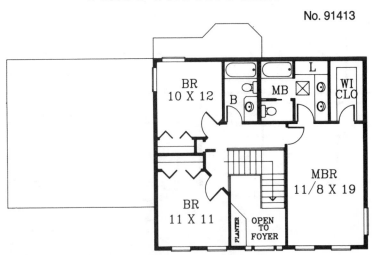

SECOND FLOOR PLAN

Family Home Features Private Bedroom Tower

No. 34049

Sloping ceilings and open spaces characterize this four-bedroom home. The dining room off the foyer adjoins the breakfast room and the convenient island kitchen. The beamed living room is crowned by a balcony overlook that links the upstairs bedrooms. The vaulted first-floor master suite features a private deck, a walk-in closet and a full bath with a double vanity.

First floor — 1,496 sq. ft.
Second floor — 520 sq. ft.
Basement — 1,487 sq. ft.
Garage — 424 sq. ft.

Total living area — 2,016 sq. ft.

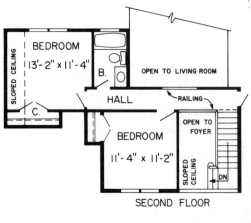

SECOND FLOOR

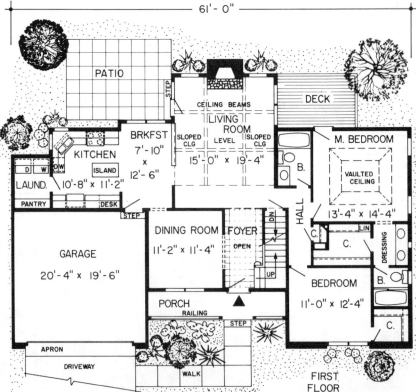

No. 34049

Elegant Design
Offers Special Living

No. 10521

This well-crafted design features four bedrooms, three baths and a balcony overlooking the two-story foyer. The master suite includes a five-piece bath, an oversized walk-in closet and a separate linen closet. The kitchen has a breakfast nook and includes both a desk and pantry. The formal living room with fireplace has direct access to the rear deck.

First floor — 1,191 sq. ft.
Second floor — 699 sq. ft.
Basement — 1,191 sq. ft.
Garage — 454 sq. ft.

Total living area — 1,890 sq. ft.

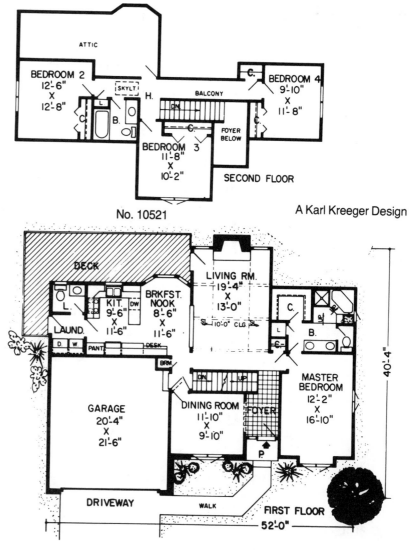

No. 10521

A Karl Kreeger Design

Contemporary Design Features Sunken Living Room

No. 26112

Wood adds its warmth to the contemporary features of this passive solar design. Generous use of southern glass doors and windows, an air lock entry, skylights and a living room fireplace reduce energy needs. R-26 insulation is used for floors and sloping ceilings. Decking rims the front of the home and gives access through sliding glass doors to a bedroom-den area and living room. The dining room lies up several steps from the living room and is separated from it by a half wall. The dining room flows into the kitchen through an eating bar. A second floor landing balcony overlooks the living room. Two bedrooms, one with its own private deck, and a full bath finish the second level.

First floor — 911 sq. ft.
Second floor — 576 sq. ft.
Basement — 911 sq. ft.

Total living area — 1,487 sq. ft.

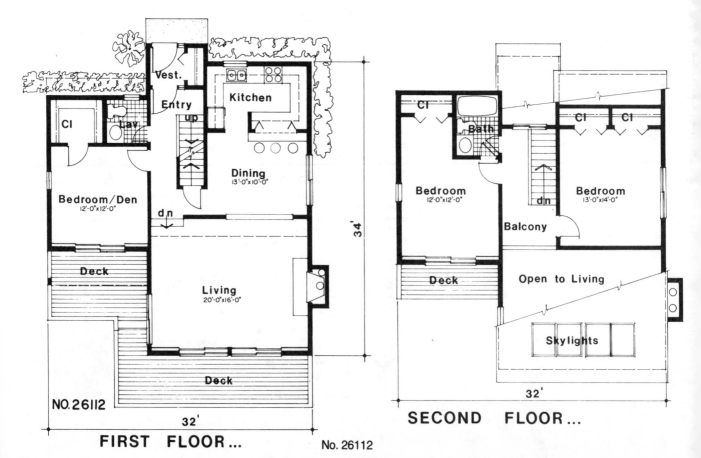

NO. 26112

32'

FIRST FLOOR...   No. 26112

SECOND FLOOR...

Sunken Living Areas in Compact Plan

No. 26114

Step down from the entry-level to the sunken living, dining, and kitchen areas of this floor plan. The fireplaced living room looks out through double sliding glass doors to a wrap-around deck which ends in outside storage. Ceilings slope up above a balcony which also shares the second level with two bedrooms and a bath. An optional third bedroom/den lies on the lower level.

First floor — 696 sq. ft.
Second floor — 416 sq. ft.
Basement — 696 sq. ft.
Storage — 32 sq. ft.
Deck — 232 sq. ft.

Total living area — 1,112 sq. ft.

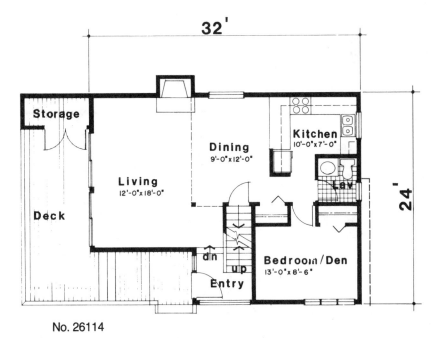

No. 26114

FIRST FLOOR

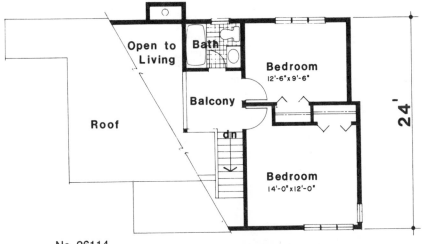

No. 26114

SECOND FLOOR

Affordable Ranch

No. 99318

This simple-to-frame ranch adds the right touches where they count the most. From the vaulted entry with garage access there is a view of the corner fireplace and rear yard through the sliding glass doors of the vaulted living and dining rooms. The kitchen opens to the living areas and overlooks the covered corner patio which can easily be screened in. The three bedrooms include one with a double door den option opening to the living room, and a full master bedroom with private full bath and walk-in closet.

Main living area — 1,159 sq. ft

Garage — 2-car

Total living area —1,159 sq. ft.

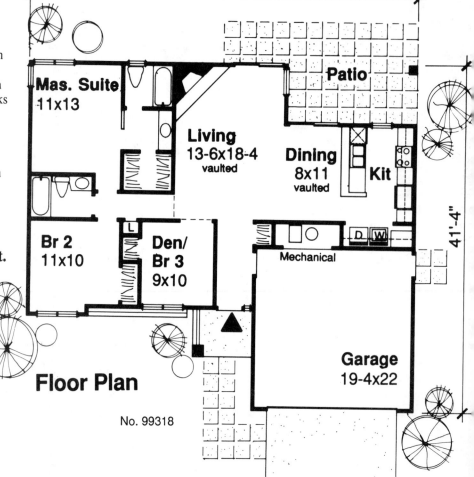

Floor Plan

No. 99318

48'-0"

41'-4"

Mas. Suite
11x13

Living
13-6x18-4
vaulted

Patio

Dining
8x11
vaulted

Kit

Br 2
11x10

Den/
Br 3
9x10

Mechanical

Garage
19-4x22

Compact Design Offers Bigger Look

No. 90370

The move-up market is demanding more than the basics: more in appearance, more in space, and more in quality equipment. This plan is designed to appeal those who want the look of a bigger house with traditional details within a contemporary compactform.

First floor — 817 sq. ft.
Second floor — 699 sq. ft.
Garage — 2-car

Total living area — 1,516 sq. ft.

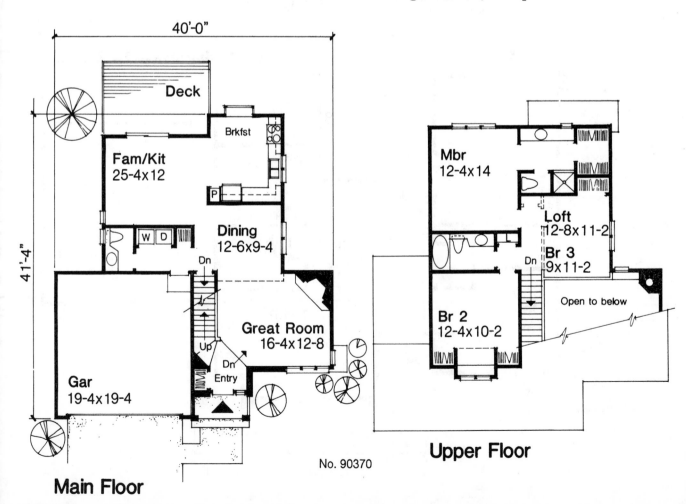

40'-0"

41'-4"

Deck

Brkfst

Fam/Kit
25-4x12

Dining
12-6x9-4

W D

P

Dn

Up

Dn
Entry

Great Room
16-4x12-8

Gar
19-4x19-4

Main Floor

No. 90370

Mbr
12-4x14

Loft
12-8x11-2

Br 3
9x11-2

Dn

Open to below

Br 2
12-4x10-2

Upper Floor

Half-Round Window Graces Attractive Exterior

No. 90395

This handsome home combines convenience and drama by adding a bedroom wing a half-level above active areas. The result of this distinctive design is a striking, spacious feeling in living spaces, along with uncompromised privacy for the two bedrooms at the rear of the house. Look at the soaring ceilings of the kitchen, living, dining, and breakfast rooms. Notice the little touches that make life easier: the private bath entrance from the master suite, the pass-through between kitchen and dining room, the built-in planning desk, the bookcases that flank the fireplace. Don't need a third bedroom? The front room on the entry level doubles as a home office or den.

Garage — 2-car

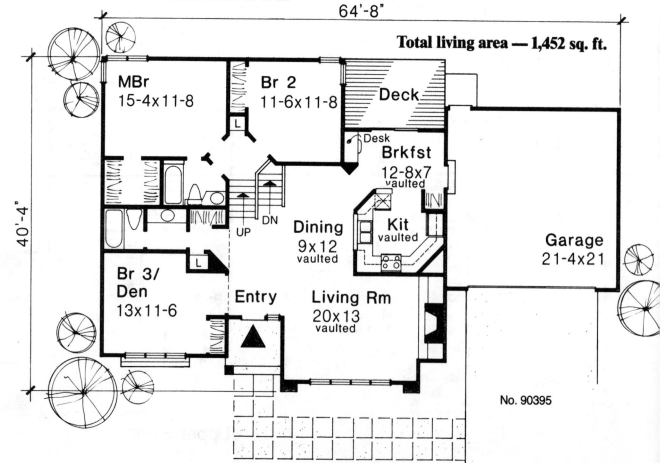

Total living area — 1,452 sq. ft.

64'-8"

40'-4"

MBr
15-4x11-8

Br 2
11-6x11-8

Deck

Desk

Brkfst
12-8x7
vaulted

Dining
9x12
vaulted

Kit
vaulted

Garage
21-4x21

DN

UP

Br 3/
Den
13x11-6

Entry

Living Rm
20x13
vaulted

No. 90395

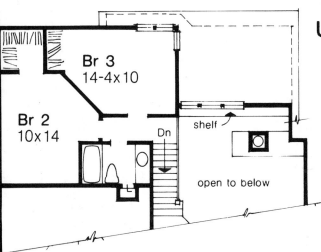

Upper Floor

First floor — 1,006 sq. ft.
Second floor — 437 sq. ft.
Garage — 2-car

Total living area — 1,443 sq. ft.

Br 3
14-4x10

Br 2
10x14

Dn

shelf

open to below

Country Contemporary

No. 90372

An inviting porch is a welcoming introduction to this compact charmer, adaptable to any lifestyle. Retirees will appreciate the first-floor master suite that eliminates stair-climbing. But, families can take advantage of the bedrooms and full bath on the upper floor. At mealtime, there are lots of choices. Eat in the U-shaped kitchen's bayed nook, the formal dining room, or the deck just beyond the sliding glass doors. And, for entertaining, or just plain relaxing, the vaulted, sunken living room with its massive fireplace and clerestory windows is a sunny, comfortable spot.

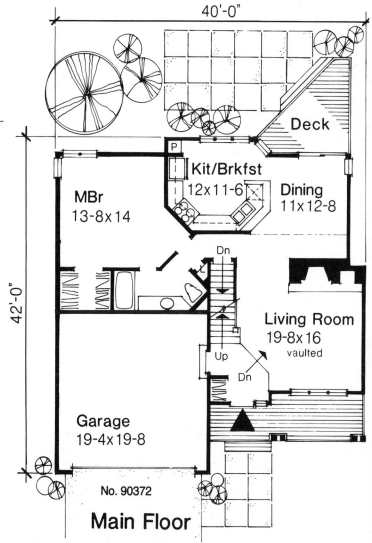

40'-0"

Deck

Kit/Brkfst
12x11-6

Dining
11x12-8

MBr
13-8x14

42'-0"

Dn

Up

Dn

Living Room
19-8x16
vaulted

Garage
19-4x19-8

No. 90372

Main Floor

Easy Living, with a Hint of Drama

No. 90676

This one-level contemporary with a rustic, farmhouse flavor combines a touch of luxury with an informal plan. Watch the world go by from your kitchen vantage point, large enough for a family meal, and conveniently located for easy service to the formal dining room. When the weather's nice, use the built-in barbecue on the covered porch, accessible through sliders in both dining and living rooms. But, when there's a chill in the air, you'll enjoy the cozy, yet spacious ambiance of the living room, with its exposed beams, crackling fire, and soaring, cathedral ceilings. You'll also appreciate the privacy of three bedrooms, down the hallway off the foyer. Hall and master baths feature convenient, split-design and double-bowl vanities.

Main living area — 1,575 sq. ft.
Garage — 2-car

Total living area — 1,575 sq. ft.

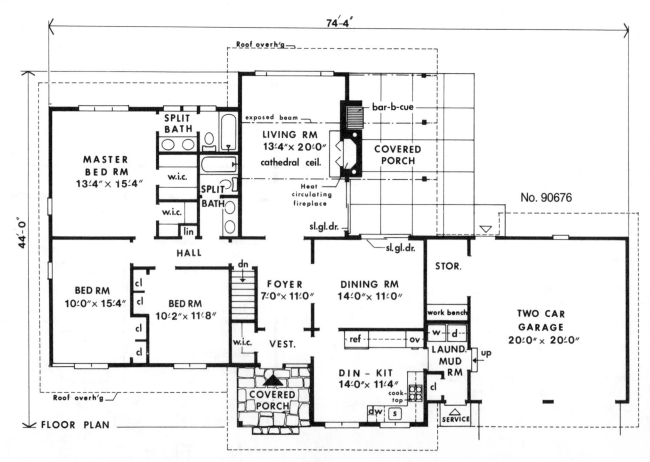

FLOOR PLAN

Face this House
South for Solar Gain

No. 90620

This modest ranch with generous rooms and passive solar features provides comfortable living for the family on a budget. The soaring, skylit central foyer provides access to every room. Straight ahead, the living room, dining room, and greenhouse form a bright, airy arrangement of glass and open space. The adjacent kitchen conveniently opens to a spacious, bay-windowed dinette. A separate wing contains three bedrooms and two baths, including an ample master suite.

Main living area — 1,405 sq. ft.
Basement — 1,415 sq. ft.

Total living area — 1,405 sq. ft.

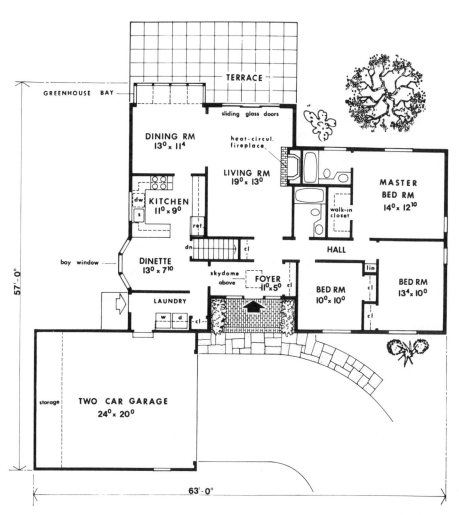

TERRACE

GREENHOUSE BAY

sliding glass doors

DINING RM
$13^0 \times 11^4$

heat-circul.
fireplace

LIVING RM
$19^0 \times 13^0$

MASTER
BED RM
$14^0 \times 12^{10}$

dw
KITCHEN
$11^0 \times 9^0$

walk-in
closet

s

ref.

HALL

dn

cl

bay window

DINETTE
$13^0 \times 7^{10}$

lin

BED RM
$13^4 \times 10^0$

skydome
above

FOYER
$11^0 \times 5^0$

cl

BED RM
$10^0 \times 10^0$

cl

LAUNDRY

w   d   cl

57'-0"

storage

TWO CAR GARAGE
$24^0 \times 20^0$

63'-0"

No. 90620

Railings Unify Open Design

No. 90900

Vaulted ceilings and open spaces highlight the interior of this delightful contemporary design, finished in horizontal cedar with a shake roof. From the moment you step into the foyer with its 2-story ceiling and skylight, you'll be impressed with the spaciousness of this plan. Every room on the main floor is zoned according to function in a step-saving arrangement. A versatile loft upstairs overlooks the living room and foyer below and provides access to three bedrooms and two baths.

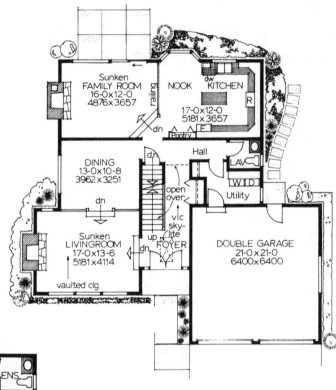

Sunken FAMILY ROOM
16-0x12-0
4876x3657

NOOK

KITCHEN
17-0x12-0
5181x3657

railing

dn

Pantry

DINING
13-0x10-8
3962x3251

Hall

LAV

W/D

Utility

dn

open over

v/c sky-lite
FOYER

Sunken LIVINGROOM
17-0x13-6
5181x4114

dn

up

DOUBLE GARAGE
21-0 x 21-0
6400x6400

vaulted clg.

BR 2
11-0x12-0
3352x3657

MBR
14-0x12-0
4267x3657

ENS

BATH

LOFT
13-4 x 8-10
4064 x 2692
railing

Hall

dn

lin

BR 3
9-0x10-10
2743x3302

No. 90900

Livingroom below

Foyer below

SECOND FLOOR PLAN

Main floor — 1,156 sq. ft.
Second floor — 808 sq. ft.
Unfinished basement —
1,160 sq. ft.
Garage — 473 sq. ft.
Width — 48'-0"
Depth — 47'- 6"

Total living area — 1,964 sq. ft.

Start With Style

No. 99333

Small starter homes get more important-looking all the time. This house is no exception. The traditional look of the house gives visual appeal, yet the texture and pattern differences lend a customized look. Inside, the visual flow gives a spacious feeling. The master bath adds to the custom feel with compartmental toilet, oversized tub/shower and walk-in closet. The house is shown with a basement, but it can easily be built on a slab or crawl space.

Main living area — 1,338 sq. ft.
Garage — 2-car

Total living area — 1,338 sq. ft.

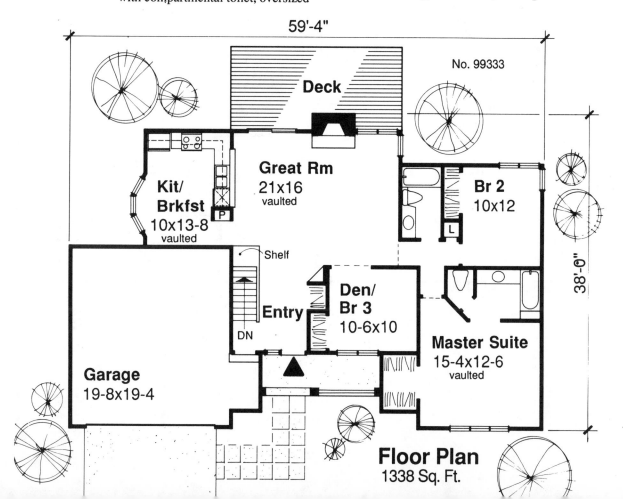

59'-4"

No. 99333

Deck

Great Rm
21x16
vaulted

Kit/
Brkfst
10x13-8
vaulted

Br 2
10x12

Shelf

Entry

Den/
Br 3
10-6x10

DN

Master Suite
15-4x12-6
vaulted

Garage
19-8x19-4

38'-0"

Floor Plan
1338 Sq. Ft.

Built-In Beauty

No. 90942

The brick and stucco exterior of this
beautiful home encloses a spacious
plan designed for convenience. A
huge, sunken living room with vaulted
ceilings flows into the formal dining
room overlooking the backyard. Eat
here, or in the nook on the other side of
the adjoining kitchen. An open railing
and a single stair separate the nook and
the fireplaced family room, each featuring sliding glass doors to the patio.
Notice the built-ins throughout the
house that help keep clutter down, and
the handy bath tucked behind the
garage. Three bedrooms up the open
staircase include the expansive master
suite with private dressing room, walk-
in closet, and double-vanitied bath with
step-in shower.

First floor — 1,175 sq. ft.
Second floor — 776 sq. ft.
Basement — 1,165 sq. ft.
Garage — 410 sq. ft.
Width — 44'-0"
Depth — 46'-6"

Total living area — 1,951 sq. ft.

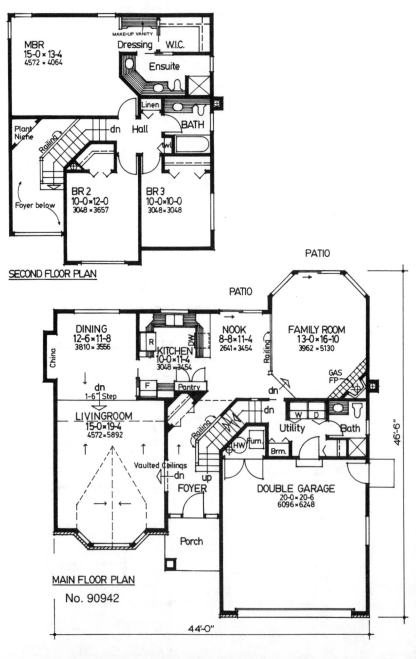

Windows And Angles Create Spectacular Views

No. 91655

This splendid, contemporary home makes creative use of a unique floor plan. From the imposing front with large windows and stunning stucco exterior, to the dramatic coved-ceilings and angular rooms, it's a dream come true. Luxuriate in the spa in the master suite or enjoy views from magnificent windows in the family and living rooms, dining nook and master bedroom.

Main floor — 1,173 sq. ft.
Upper floor — 823 sq. ft.
Bonus room — 204 sq. ft.
Garage — 2-car

Total living area — 1,996 sq. ft.

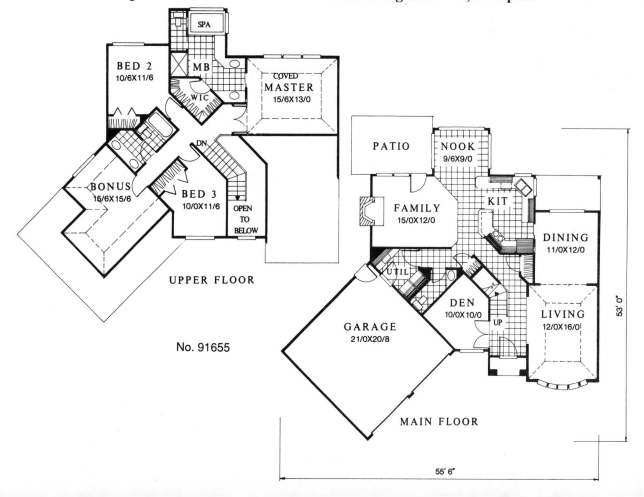

UPPER FLOOR

No. 91655

MAIN FLOOR

Arch Recalls
Another Era

No. 90675

Massive roof lines pierced with clerestory windows only hint at the interior excitement of this contemporary beauty. The vaulted foyer of this elegant home, graced by Doric columns that support an elegant arch, lends an air of ancient Greece to the spacious living and dining rooms. To the right, a well-appointed peninsula kitchen features pass-over convenience to the adjoining dinette bay and family room. Open the sliding glass doors to add an outdoor feeling to every room at the rear of the house. The ample master suite features a private terrace and whirlpool bath. A hall bath serves the other bedrooms in the sleeping wing off the entry.

Main living area — 1,558 sq. ft.
Laundry/mudroom — 97 sq. ft.
Garage — 2-car

Total living area — 1,655 sq. ft.

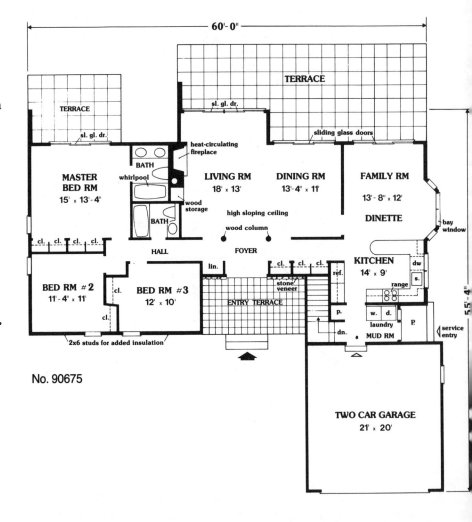

No. 90675

Overhang Provides Shade from the Noonday Sun

No. 90502

A sheltered entry opens to the airy, fireplaced living and dining room of this one-level, stucco home. Behind double doors, the family room shares a view of the deck with the kitchen and adjoining, bay-windowed breakfast nook. The window of the front bedroom, framed by a graceful arch, looks out over its own, private garden. An angular hall leads to the laundry, two additional bedrooms and two full baths.

Main living area — 1,642 sq. ft.

Garage — 2-car

Total living area — 1,642 sq. ft.

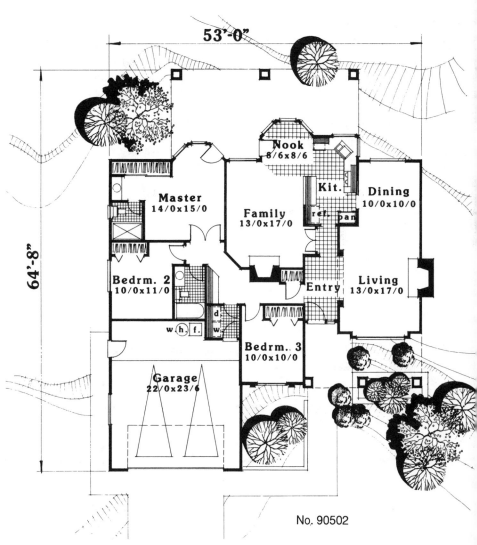

No. 90502

Inviting Porch Adorns Affordable Home

No. 90682

You don't have to give up storage space to build an affordable home. With large closets just inside the front door and in every bedroom, a walk-in pantry by the kitchen, and an extra-large storage area tucked behind the garage, you can build this house on an optional slab foundation and still keep the clutter to a minimum. The L-shaped living and dining room arrangement, brightened by triple windows and sliding glass doors, adds a spacious feeling to active areas. Eat in formal elegance overlooking the patio, or have a family meal in the country kitchen. Tucked in a private wing for quiet bedtime atmosphere, three bedrooms and two full baths complete this affordable home loaded with amenities.

Main living area — 1,160 sq. ft.
Garage — 2-car

Total living area — 1,160 sq. ft.

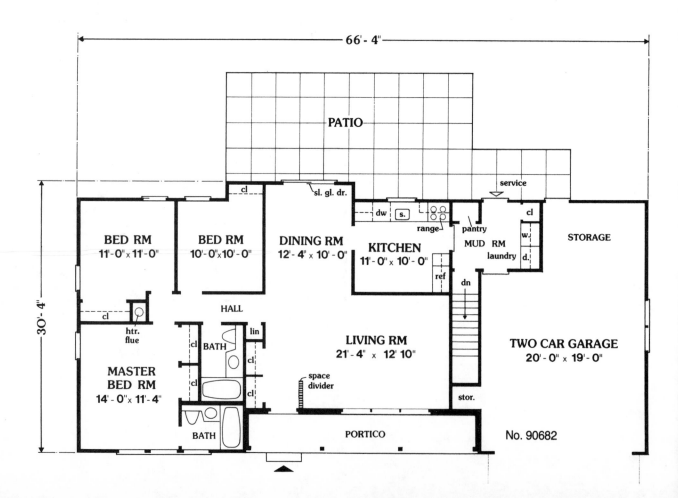

Dutch Colonial Accent

No. 90686

Face the rear of this one-level home south to take advantage of the warmth and light you'll gain through its abundant windows and sliding glass doors. Its sunny atmosphere is accentuated by a greenhouse bay in the dining room, and a skylight piercing the soaring ceiling of the spacious living room. You'll appreciate the central kitchen location whether you're serving a formal dinner, a barbecue on the terrace, or popcorn in the family room. A hallway off the foyer leads past a full bath to three bedrooms. The rear-facing master suite includes a walk-in closet and private bath with double vanities and a whirlpool tub. Build this home with or without a basement and there's lots of storage space in the garage.

Main living area — 1,544 sq. ft.
Laundry/mudroom — 74 sq. ft.
Garage/storage — 516 sq. ft.

Total living area — 1,618 sq. ft.

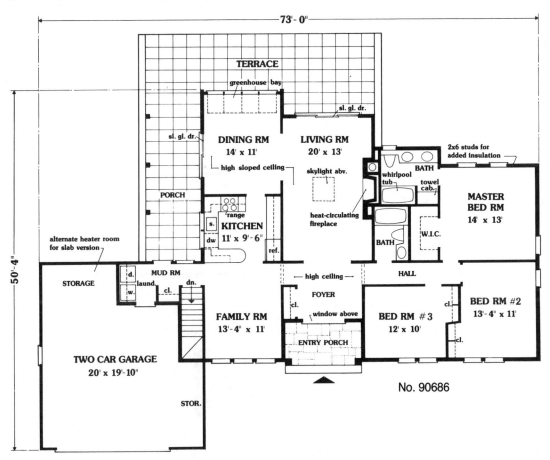

No. 90686

Year Round Retreat

No. 90613

This compact home is a bargain to build and designed to save on energy bills. Large glass areas face south, and the dramatic sloping ceiling of the living room allows heat from the wood-burning stove to rise into the upstairs bedrooms through high louvers on the inside wall. In hot weather, just open the windows on both floors for cooling air circulation. Sliding glass doors in the kitchen and living room open to the deck for outdoor dining or relaxation. One bedroom and a full bath complete the first floor. A stair off the foyer ends in a balcony with a commanding view of the living room. Two spacious bedrooms are separated by a full bath.

First floor — 917 sq. ft.
Second floor — 465 sq. ft.
(optional slab construction available)

Total living area — 1,382 sq. ft.

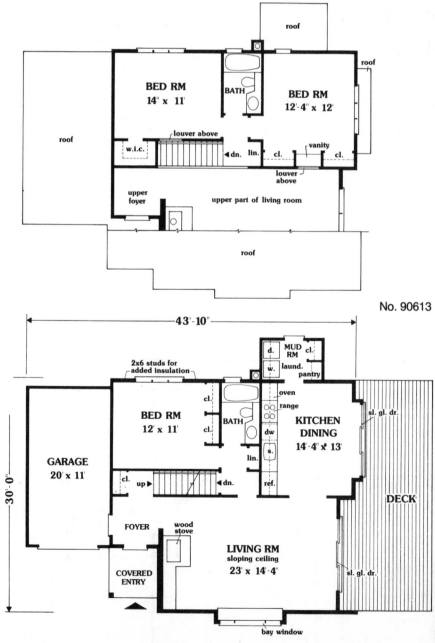

No. 90613

Living Room Focus of Spacious Home

No. 10328

Equipped with fireplace and sliding glass doors to the bordering deck, the two-story living room creates a sizeable and airy center for family activity. A well-planned traffic pattern connects the dining area, kitchen, laundry niche

and bath. Closets are plentiful, and a total of three 15-foot bedrooms are shown. A balcony overlooking the open living room is featured on the second floor.

First floor — 1,024 sq. ft.
Second floor — 576 sq. ft.
Basement — 1,024 sq. ft.

Total living area — 1,600 sq. ft.

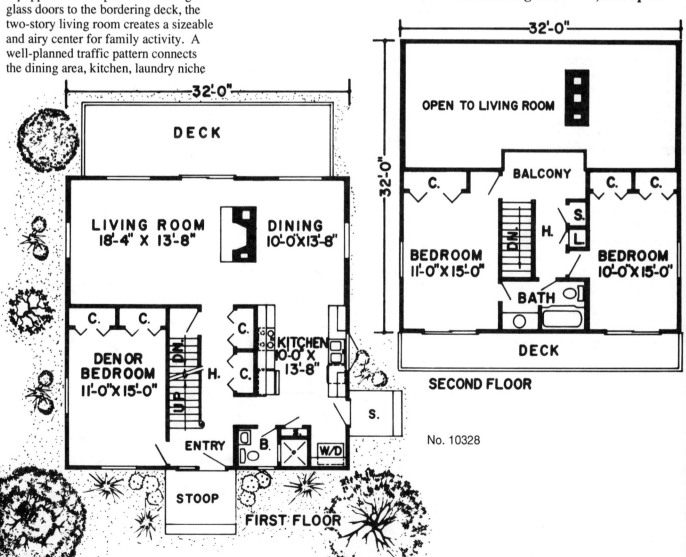

32'-0"

DECK

LIVING ROOM 18'-4" X 13'-8"

DINING 10'-0"X13'-8"

C. C.

DEN OR BEDROOM 11'-0"X15'-0"

C.

C.

UP DN.

H.

KITCHEN 10'-0" X 13'-8"

S.

ENTRY

B.

W/D

STOOP

FIRST FLOOR

32'-0"

32'-0"

OPEN TO LIVING ROOM

C.

BALCONY

C. C.

S.

BEDROOM 11'-0"X15'-0"

DN.

H.

L.

BEDROOM 10'-0"X15'-0"

BATH

DECK

SECOND FLOOR

No. 10328

For A European Look

No. 90446

The stucco exterior gives a European flair to this Traditional floor plan. The large Great room with fireplace has a wood deck to its rear. The breakfast room with its bay window is conveniently located behind the galley-style kitchen. The large dining room is perfect for formal dinners. The upstairs master suite has a walk-in closet and a separate bath with tub and shower. The other bedrooms and second full bath complete the second floor. The unfinished room over the garage can be finished for extra space. Please specify basement or crawlspace when ordering.

First floor — 1,048 sq. ft.
Second floor — 1,050 sq. ft.
Opt. bonus room — 284 sq. ft.
Basement — 1,034 sq. ft.
Garage — 2-car

Total living area — 2,098 sq. ft.

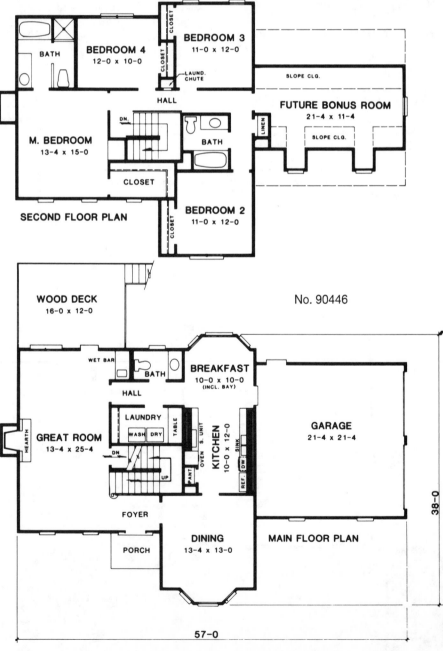

Compact Two Story Has Victorian Flair

No. 90445

This two-story Traditional has room for many residents. The large Great room has a fireplace plus a view of the open stair. The dining room features a boxed window, and leads into the galley-style kitchen. The breakfast nook with bay window is adjacent to the garage and outdoor deck. The guest room with a full bath is perfect for company. Upstairs the master suite has a tray ceiling and convenient media center. The master bath features a corner tub and walk-in closet, as well as a separate shower. Two other bedrooms and another full bath complete the second floor. The optional bonus room over the garage can serve as another bedroom or playroom. The plan is available with either basement, crawl-space or slab foundation. Please specify when ordering.

Main floor — 1,030 sq. ft.
Second floor — 1,020 sq. ft.
Bonus room — 284 sq. ft.

Total living area — 2,050 sq. ft.

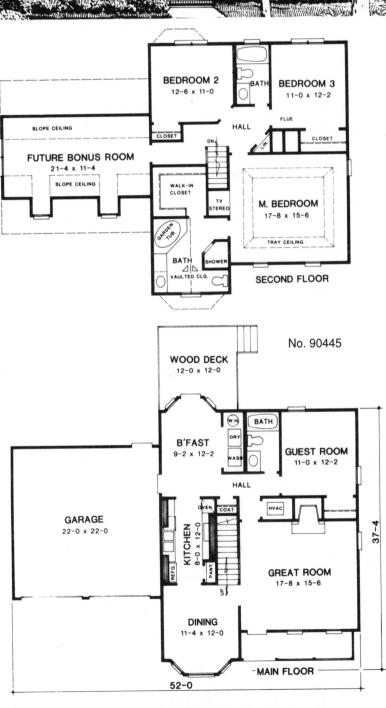

BEDROOM 2
12-6 x 11-0

BATH

BEDROOM 3
11-0 x 12-2

SLOPE CEILING

CLOSET

HALL

FLUE

DN.

LIN.

CLOSET

FUTURE BONUS ROOM
21-4 x 11-4

SLOPE CEILING

WALK-IN CLOSET

TV STEREO

M. BEDROOM
17-8 x 15-6

GARDEN TUB

BATH

SHOWER

VAULTED CLG.

TRAY CEILING

SECOND FLOOR

No. 90445

WOOD DECK
12-0 x 12-0

W.H.

BATH

DRY

B'FAST
9-2 x 12-2

WASH

GUEST ROOM
11-0 x 12-2

HALL

OVEN

COAT

HVAC

GARAGE
22-0 x 22-0

KITCHEN
8-0 x 12-0

PANT.

UP

REFG.

GREAT ROOM
17-8 x 15-6

37-4

DINING
11-4 x 12-0

MAIN FLOOR

52-0

Street Appeal

No. 91802

Striking street appeal is enhanced by the quarter round windows and soldier courses of brick. The gentle mix of hip and gable roofs blend together setting the standards for the neighborhood. Inside multi-sloping ceilings flow from the foyer into the living room. The formal dining room features a buffet counter. The kitchen provides plenty of cabinets along with a pantry and eating bar. The nook and sunken family room are open to the kitchen keeping the family together. Adjacent to the two-car garage is a large utility room with an abundance of cabinet and counter space. The master suite features a walk-in closet and double sinks in the dressing area along with a toilet and shower privately located in a seperate room. Two spare bedrooms and another full bath round out the balance of this home. Please specify basement, slab or crawlspace foundation when ordering.

Main floor — 1,871 sq. ft.
Garage — 2-car

Total living area - 1,871 Sq. Ft.

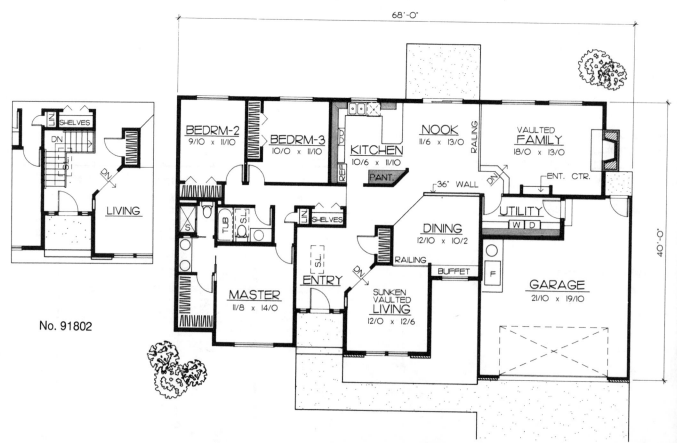

No. 91802

Efficient Compact Design

No. 91641

This deceptively simple dwelling boasts many features normally found only in much larger homes. There are three bedrooms, two baths, a generous-sized utility room, and a modern kitchen with a separate pantry. The master suite features his-and-her sinks in the bathroom and a walk-in closet, while storage space abounds on all sides. This plan is a power-packed 1,418 square feet.

Main living area — 1,418 sq. ft.
Garage — 2-car

Total living area — 1,418 sq. ft.

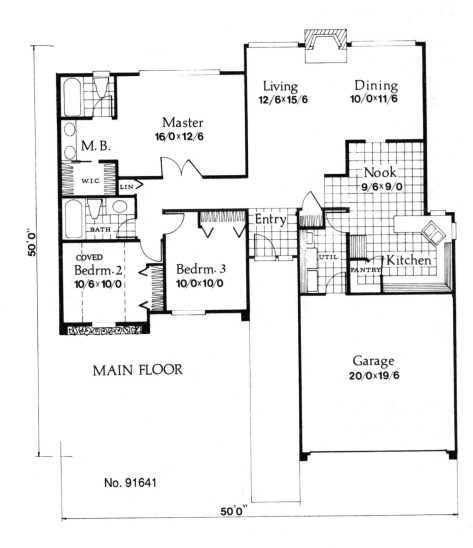

Living 12/6×15/6

Dining 10/0×11/6

Master 16/0×12/6

M. B.

W.I.C.

LIN

Nook 9/6×9/0

BATH

Entry

UTIL

Kitchen

COVED Bedrm. 2 10/6×10/0

Bedrm. 3 10/0×10/0

PANTRY

50'0"

MAIN FLOOR

Garage 20/0×19/6

No. 91641

50'0"

Design Features Six Ideas

No. 1074

Simple lines flow from this six-sided design. It's affordably scaled, but sizable enough for a growing family. Active living areas are snuggled centrally between two quiet bedroom and bath areas in the floor plan. A small hallway, leading to two bedrooms and a full bath on the right side, may be completely shut off from the living room, providing seclusion. Another bath lies behind a third bedroom on the left side, complete with washer/dryer facilities and close enough to a stoop and rear entrance to serve as a mudroom.

Main living area — 1,040 sq. ft.
Storage — 44 sq. ft.
Deck — 258 sq. ft.
Carport — 230 sq. ft.

Total living area — 1,040 sq. ft.

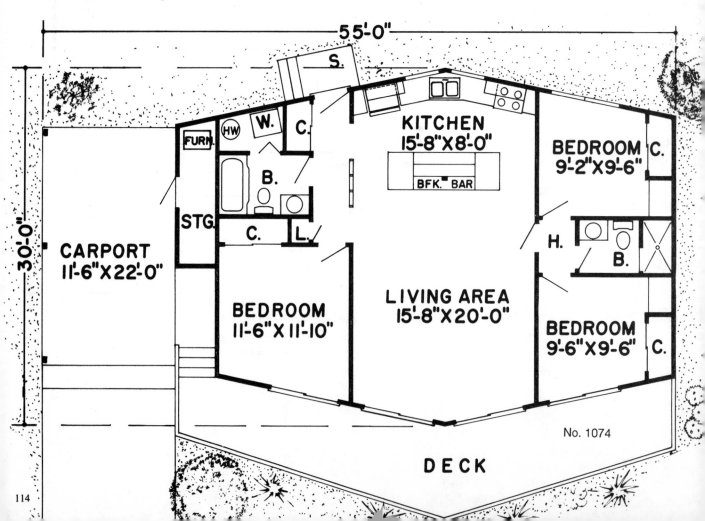

55'-0"

30'-0"

S.

FURN. HW W. C.

B.

STG. C. L.

CARPORT
11'-6"X 22'-0"

BEDROOM
11'-6" X 11'-10"

KITCHEN
15'-8"X8'-0"

BFK. BAR

LIVING AREA
15'-8"X20'-0"

BEDROOM
9'-2"X9'-6" C.

H. B.

BEDROOM
9'-6"X9'-6" C.

No. 1074

DECK

Vacation Retreat Suits Year-round Living

No. 1078

A long central hallway divides formal from informal areas, assuring privacy for the two bedrooms located in the rear. Also located along the central portion of the design are a utility room and neighboring bath. The furnace, water heater and washer/dryer units are housed in the utility room. An open living/dining room area with exposed beams, sloping ceilings and optional fireplace occupies the front. Two pairs of sliding glass doors access the large deck from this area. The house may also be entered from the carport on the right or the deck on the left.

First floor — 1,024 sq. ft.
Carport & storage — 387 sq. ft.
Deck — 411 sq. ft.

Total living area — 1,024 sq. ft.

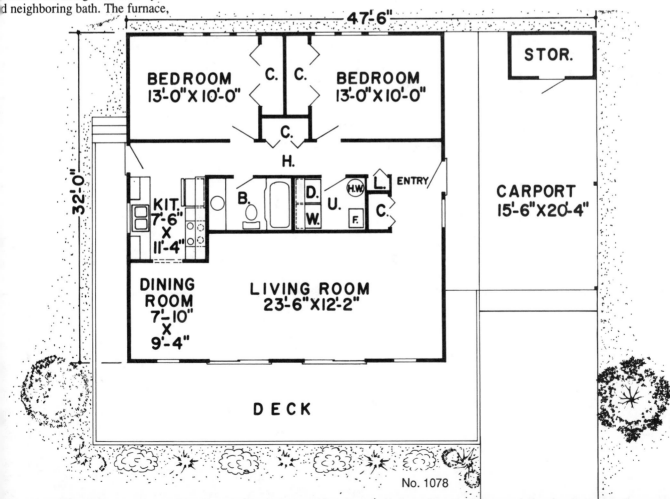

No. 1078

Excellent First Home

No. 28015

Solar storage cells on the south side contribute to the energy-saving effectiveness of this well-designed beginning family home. Three bedrooms and two baths occupy the east wing. The master bedroom features a large walk-in closet and private bath. The Great room opens out onto a patio while the kitchen gives access to the large double garage. A breakfast bar separates the kitchen from the living area while giving the feeling of spacious and open living. An air-lock entry adds to the energy-saving features.

Main living area — 1,296 sq. ft.
Garage — 484 sq. ft.

Total living area — 1,296 sq. ft.

No. 28015

C.

BEDROOM 11'-7" X 11'-4"

BEDROOM 11'-4" X 11'-4"

C.

GREAT ROOM 21'-3" X 11'-5"

C.

BEDROOM 12'-10" X 11'-4"

BATH

BATH

ENTRY

UTILITY

KITCHEN 15'-0" X 11'-4"

GARAGE 21'-4" X 21'-8"

51'-0"

46'-0"

Compact Charmer
No. 10789

From its traditional covered porch to its wide-open interior, this house is loaded with warmth and charm. A central foyer separates active and quiet areas. To the left, tucked behind the garage, three bedrooms and two full baths include the spacious master suite with its sunny bay sitting area and private patio access. You'll find another bay just off the family room, a perfect place to watch the birds as you wake up with your morning coffee. Clean up chores won't be dull in the centrally-located kitchen with its corner sink surrounded by windows. And just steps away, the open living and dining rooms span the width of the house in a sunny, spacious arrangement that's ideal for entertaining.

Main living area — 1,692 sq. ft.
Garage — sq. ft.

Total living area — 1,692 sq. ft.

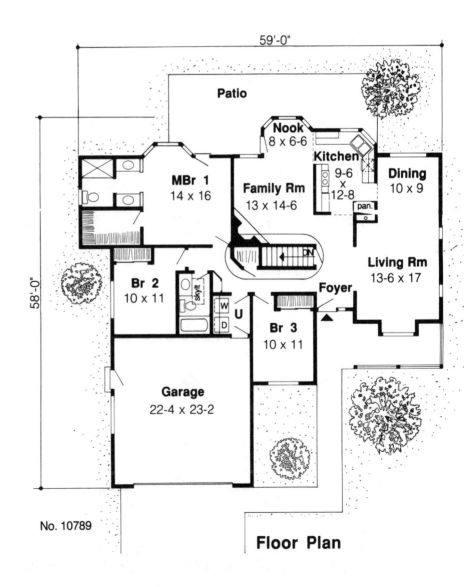

No. 10789

Floor Plan

Comfortable Cottage Suits Narrow Lot

No. 8082

Adaptable to a 50-foot lot, this small cottage boasts an exterior of horizontal siding, brick, and shutters, as well as a cozy interior. Entry is directly into the living room, splashed with light from the plentiful windows. Large enough to entertain a group of people, the living room is shut off from sleeping quarters by a door, which encourages maximum privacy and quiet. Two adequate bedrooms and a full bath are set opposite an extra storage closet.

Main living area — 936 sq. ft.
Basement — 936 sq. ft.

Total living area — 936 sq. ft.

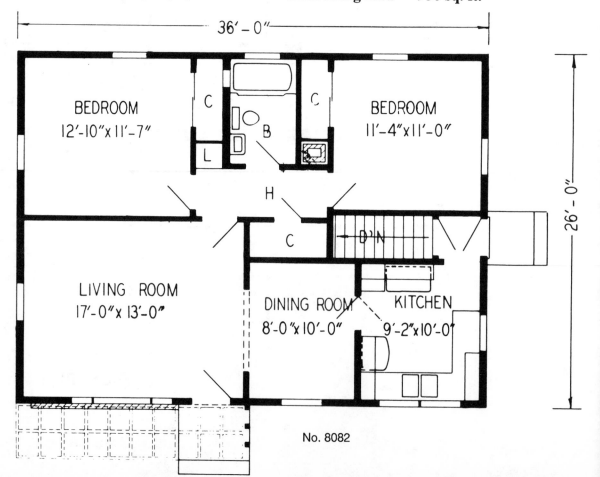

No. 8082

Affordable Amenities

No. 10794

This home offers convenience, charm, and the amenities you've been looking for, in an attractive plan that won't break your building budget. Look at all the features that make life easier: one-floor living for easy cleaning, a large, built-in pantry off the dining room, an efficient U-shaped kitchen, a separate laundry, and handy garage entry. And the special touches — like a private bath in the corner master suite, another hall bath that serves the two back bedrooms, and sliding glass doors that brighten the dining room adjoining the spacious living room, make this a home your family will cherish for years to come.

Main living area — 1,400 sq. ft.
Optional garage — 528 sq. ft.

Total living area — 1,400 sq. ft.

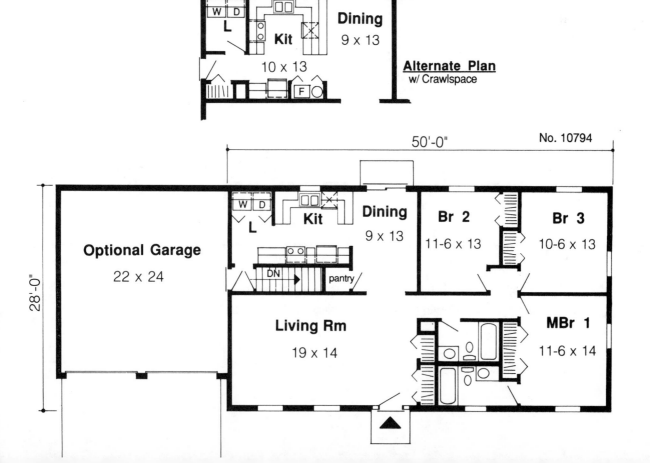

Graceful Porch Enhances Charm

No. 90106

The formal living room which is sheltered by the railed porch may be used only for company because of the multi-functional kitchen, dining and family room which are immediately behind it. This "three-rooms-in-one" design is easily adaptable to any number of lifestyles. Adjacent to the open kitchen with its efficient design and ample counter space is the hobby area that includes laundry facilities. Of the three large bedrooms, the master bedroom features a walk-in closet and private bath.

Main living area — 1,643 sq. ft.
Garage — 2-car

Total living area — 1,643 sq. ft.

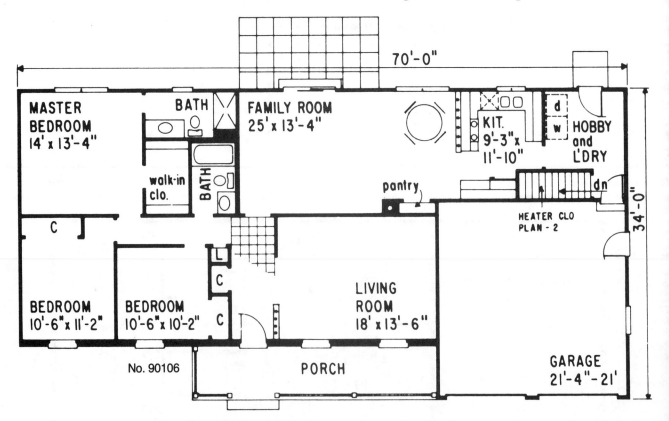

MASTER BEDROOM 14' x 13'-4"

BATH

FAMILY ROOM 25' x 13'-4"

KIT. 9'-3"x 11'-10"

HOBBY and L'DRY

walk-in clo.

BATH

pantry

dn

HEATER CLO PLAN - 2

c

BEDROOM 10'-6"x 11'-2"

BEDROOM 10'-6"x10'-2"

c

c

LIVING ROOM 18' x 13'-6"

No. 90106

PORCH

GARAGE 21'-4" - 21'

70'-0"

34'-0"

Tudor Sun Catcher

No. 90249

Face the rear of this efficient ranch home south to take advantage of the sun's free energy. The breakfast room and the soaring living and dining rooms feature rear-facing glass walls, providing a sunny atmosphere enhanced by the warmth of a massive fireplace. The attached covered porch, accessible to both living and breakfast rooms, adds to the outdoor ambiance. The centrally located kitchen features a handy snack bar and built-in pantry and planning desk, just steps away from the storage area off the attached garage. You'll love the cheerful atmosphere in the three front-facing bedrooms, which share a private corner of the house with two full baths.

Main living area — 1,584 sq. ft.
Garage — 2-car

Total living area — 1,584 sq. ft.

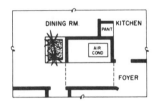

OPTIONAL NON-BASEMENT

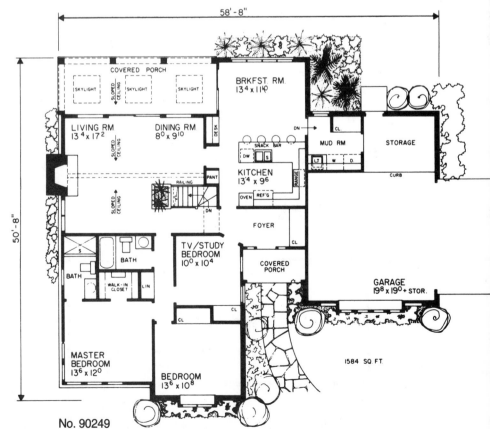

No. 90249

Carefree Convenience

No. 10674

One-level living is a breeze in this attractive, three bedroom beauty designed with your budget in mind. The covered porch adds a romantic touch to the clapboard facade. Step through the front door into a huge living room. Active areas surrounding a spacious patio at the rear of the house are served by a centrally-located galley kitchen. Eat in the formal dining room, or the handy breakfast room that adjoins the huge family room. A short hall leads to a handy full bath and two bedrooms. The master suite, tucked off the living room, features double closets and vanities for early-morning convenience.

Main living area — 1,600 sq. ft.
Garage — 465 sq. ft.

Total living area — 1,600 sq. ft.

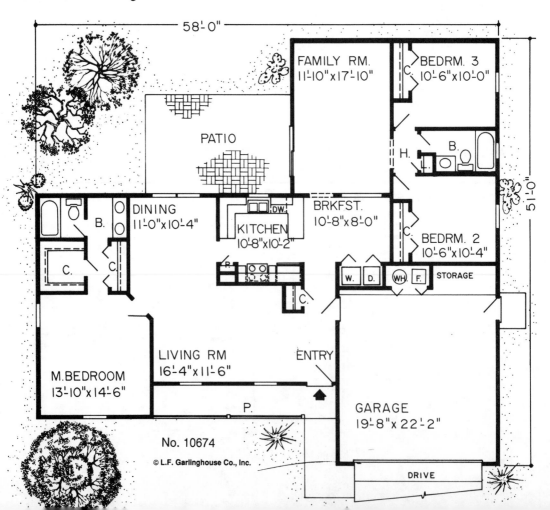

No. 10674

© L.F. Garlinghouse Co., Inc.

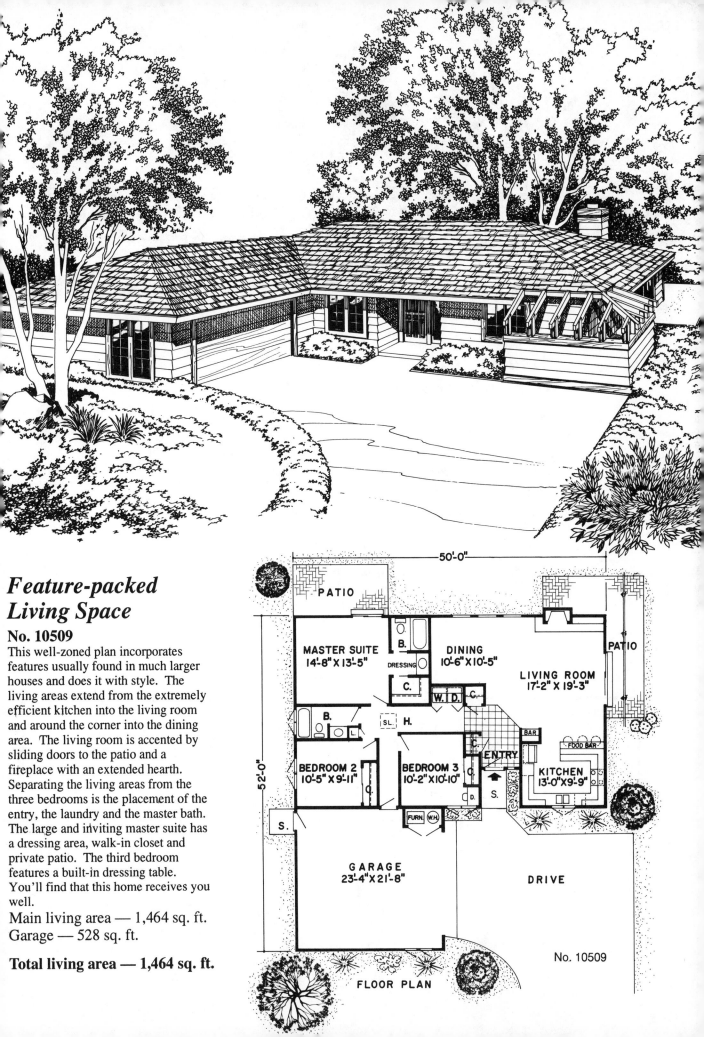

Feature-packed Living Space

No. 10509

This well-zoned plan incorporates features usually found in much larger houses and does it with style. The living areas extend from the extremely efficient kitchen into the living room and around the corner into the dining area. The living room is accented by sliding doors to the patio and a fireplace with an extended hearth. Separating the living areas from the three bedrooms is the placement of the entry, the laundry and the master bath. The large and inviting master suite has a dressing area, walk-in closet and private patio. The third bedroom features a built-in dressing table. You'll find that this home receives you well.

Main living area — 1,464 sq. ft.
Garage — 528 sq. ft.

Total living area — 1,464 sq. ft.

50'-0"

PATIO

MASTER SUITE
14'-8" X 13'-5"

B.

DRESSING

C.

DINING
10'-6" X 10'-5"

PATIO

LIVING ROOM
17'-2" X 19'-3"

W. D.

C.

52'-0"

B.

L.

SL.

H.

C.

BAR

FOOD BAR

BEDROOM 2
10'-5" X 9'-11"

BEDROOM 3
10'-2" X 10'-10"

ENTRY

KITCHEN
13'-0" X 9'-9"

C.

D.

S.

FURN.

W.H.

S.

GARAGE
23'-4" X 21'-8"

DRIVE

No. 10509

FLOOR PLAN

Window Boxes Add Romantic Charm

No. 90684

Practical yet pretty, this ranch home separates active and quiet areas for privacy when you want it. To the left, off the central foyer, you'll find a formal living and dining room combination that's just perfect for entertaining. The wing to the right of the foyer includes three spacious bedrooms and two full baths. Sunlight and warmth pervade the open, informal areas at the rear of the house, where the kitchen, dining bay, and family room

enjoy the benefits of a large fireplace and an expansive glass wall overlooking the patio. When the kids come home after a day's play, you'll appreciate the convenient lavatory location just inside the back door. There's plenty of storage space in the garage, just past the mudroom off the kitchen.

Main living area — 1,486 sq. ft.
Garage — 2-car

Total living area — 1,486 sq. ft.

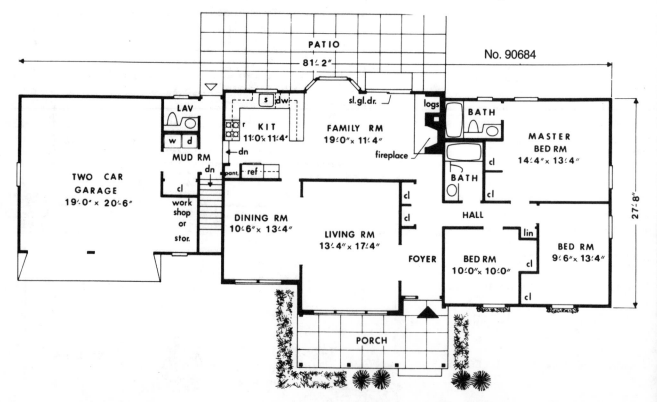

Zoned for Comfort

No. 90610

This ground-hugging ranch was designed for maximum use of the three basic living areas. The informal area —fireplaced family room, kitchen, and breakfast room— adjoins a covered porch. The fully-equipped kitchen is easily accessible to the formal dining room, which flows into the living room for convenient entertaining. Well-situated closets and bathrooms set the bedrooms apart from more active areas. The spacious master suite includes plenty of closet space and its own bath. The other bedrooms are served by the lavish hall bath equipped with two basins.

Main living area — 1,772 sq. ft.
Garage — 2-car

Total living area — 1,772 sq. ft.

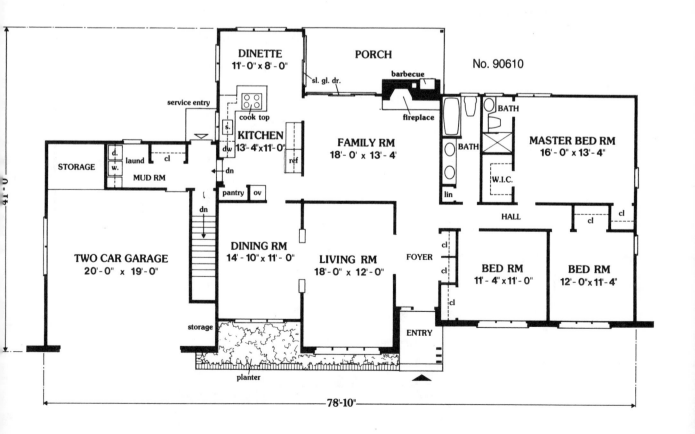

Tradition Combines With Contemporary

No. 99327

Traditional design elements such as half-round glass divider sash, covered front-entry porch, gable louvre detail, and wrap-around plant shelf under corner windows all help to create nostalgic appeal. A dramatic view awaits guests at the entry with a vaulted ceiling above the living room with clerestory glass, fireplace corner windows with half-round transom, and a long view through the dining room sliders to the rear deck. The main floor master suite has corner windows, walk-in closet and private bath access.

First floor — 858 sq. ft.
Second floor — 431 sq. ft.
Basement — 858 sq. ft.
Garage — 2-car

Total living area — 1,289 sq. ft.

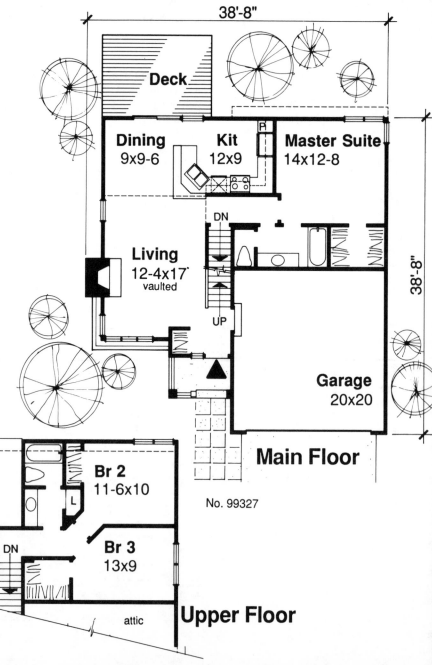

38'-8"

Deck

Dining
9x9-6

Kit
12x9

Master Suite
14x12-8

DN

Living
12-4x17
vaulted

UP

38'-8"

Garage
20x20

Main Floor

No. 99327

Br 2
11-6x10

open to below

DN

Br 3
13x9

attic

Upper Floor

Lattice Trim Adds Nostalgic Charm

No. 99315

Thanks to vaulted ceilings and an ingenious plan, this wood and fieldstone classic feels much larger than its compact size. The entry, dominated by a skylit staircase to the bedroom floor, opens to the vaulted living room with a balcony view and floor-to-ceiling corner window treatment. Eat in the spacious, formal dining room, in the sunny breakfast nook off the kitchen, or, when the weather's nice, out on the adjoining deck. Pass-through convenience makes meal service easy wherever you choose to dine. A full bath at the top of the stairs serves the kids' bedrooms off the balcony hall. The master suite boasts its own, private bath, along with a private dressing area.

First floor — 668 sq. ft.
Second floor — 691 sq. ft.
Garage — 2-car

Total living area — 1,359 sq. ft.

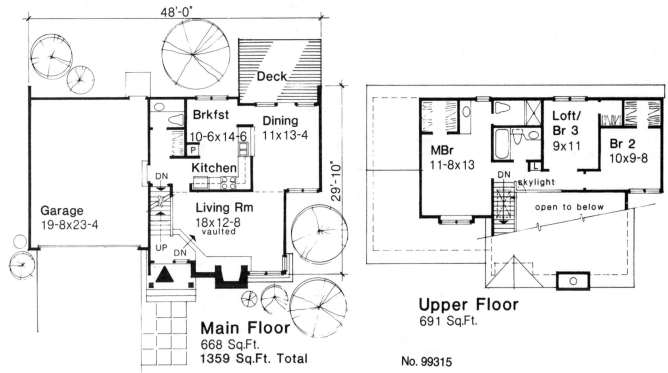

Main Floor
668 Sq.Ft.
1359 Sq.Ft. Total

48'-0"
29'-10"

Deck
Brkfst 10-6x14-6
Dining 11x13-4
Kitchen
P
Living Rm 18x12-8 vaulted
Garage 19-8x23-4
DN
UP DN

Upper Floor
691 Sq.Ft.

MBr 11-8x13
Loft/ Br 3 9x11
Br 2 10x9-8
DN skylight
open to below

No. 99315

Decorative Detailing Adds Charm

No. 34005

The covered entrance of this classy home adds a touch of charm and elegance. The living room features a cozy fireplace set between two windows and sloped ceiling. Off the living room is the kitchen equipped with a plant shelf, perfect for growing a fresh herb garden. A patio is accessible through sliding glass doors, providing a quiet escape from everyday life confusion. The dining room features a beautifully-designed ceiling enhancing formal occassions. Up a few stairs, pass an octagonal window, is the sleeping wing. The master bedroom, also featuring a decorative ceiling, has a private bath and linen closet. A second bath is equipped with washer and dryer, located across the hall from the other two bedrooms. Please indicate crawl space or basement when ordering.

Main living area — 1,441 sq. ft.
Garage — 672 sq. ft.

Total living area — 1,441 sq. ft.

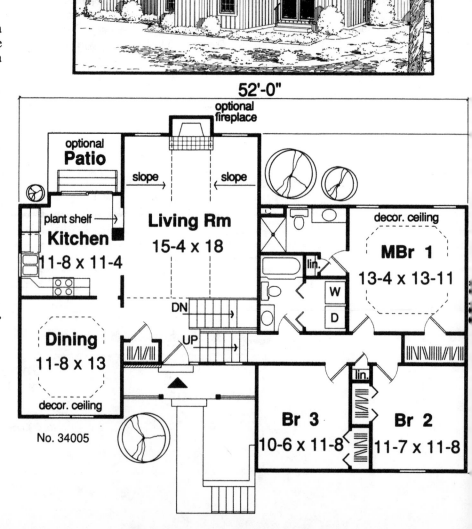

52'-0"

optional fireplace

optional **Patio**

slope   slope

plant shelf →

Kitchen
11-8 x 11-4

Living Rm
15-4 x 18

decor. ceiling

lin.

MBr 1
13-4 x 13-11

W
D

DN

Dining
11-8 x 13

UP

lin.

decor. ceiling

Br 3
10-6 x 11-8

Br 2
11-7 x 11-8

No. 34005

Cozy and Restful

No. 20195

The focus of this cozy home is on the first floor, but there is room for the children and their friends to gather in the lower-level family room which includes a fireplace and a powder room. The main floor features the living room, the dining room, the kitchen and a master bedroom with a decorative ceiling. There are also two additional bedrooms and a full bathroom with a skylight on the main floor. The washer and dryer are conveniently located outside the kitchen. The deck off the dining room can be used for outside eating if desired. This two-level is perfect for a hillside lot. This house is a cozy family retreat. The two-car garage has a lower level entrance.

Upper level — 1,139 sq. ft.
Lower level — 288 sq. ft.
Garage — 598 sq. ft.

Total living area — 1,427 sq. ft.

No. 20195

Utility

Garage
22 x 25-4

Family Rm
14 x 16

UP

Lower Level

A Karl Kreeger Design

Deck

decor. ceiling

MBr 1
14 x 11-4

skylt.

slope

Kit
10-4 x 8-4

slope

Dining
10-8 x 10

W D

9'-0" ceiling height

28'-0"

Br 2
10 x 11-8

Br 3
10 x 11-8

DN

Living Rm
14-4 x 15

Upper Level

42'-0"

The Illusion of Spaciousness

No. 91726

Multi-paned windows in the entryway, and cedar scales beneath the gable add street appeal to this tri-level. Vaulted ceilings add to the sense of spaciousness in combined living room/dining room. The fireplace adds warmth and visual interest. The dining room and kitchen are partially separated by an eating bar. Other kitchen conveniences include lazy susan shelving in a corner cupboard, and a step-in pantry that allows the stocking of kitchen shelves from behind. Utilities are close by, half a flight down, in a room they share with a toilet, lavatory and a built-in counter. Off the family room, sliding glass doors open onto a patio. The master suite has sliding glass doors that open onto a private balcony overlooking the backyard. Other amenities include a large walk-in closet and a private bathroom. The two other bedrooms face the street and share a bathroom with a tub.

First floor — 960 sq. ft.
Second floor — 768 sq. ft.
Garage — 576 sq. ft.
Width — 50'-0"
Depth — 37'-0"

Total living area — 1,728 sq. ft.

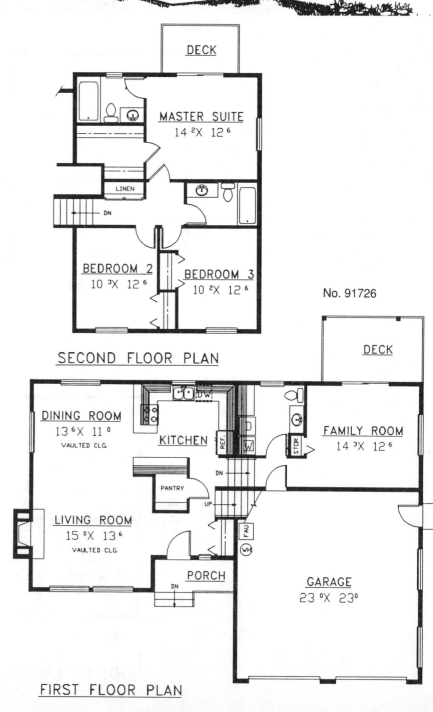

SECOND FLOOR PLAN

FIRST FLOOR PLAN

Outdoor-Lover's Dream

No. 20055

Here's a handsome home that presents a pretty face to passers-by, and provides lots of outdoor living space on a spacious rear deck. Soaring ceilings, oversized windows, and sliding glass doors unite the living room with the deck and rear yard. And, the handy kitchen makes meal service a breeze to the dining room, adjoining breakfast bay, or deck. Tucked upstairs for quiet and privacy, three bedrooms open to a skylit hallway. The dramatic master suite features soaring ceilings and a private dressing area flanked by a full bath and walk-in closet.

First floor — 928 sq. ft.
Second floor — 773 sq. ft.
Basement — 910 sq. ft.
Garage — 484 sq. ft.

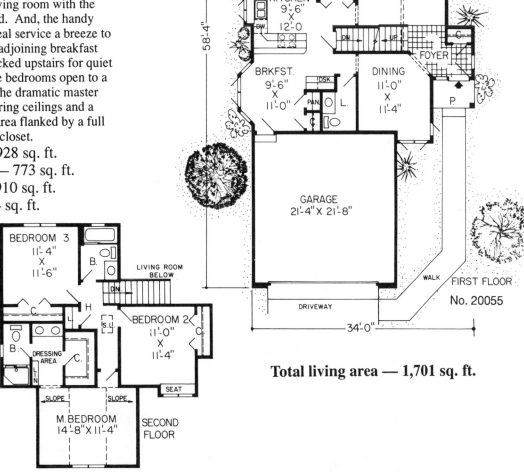

A Karl Kreeger Design

DECK

LIVING RM.
13'-4" X 19'-8"

KITCHEN
9'-6" X 12'-0

W. D.

58'-4"

BRKFST.
9'-6" X 11'-0"

DESK

PAN.

L.

C.

FOYER

DINING
11'-0" X 11'-4"

P.

GARAGE
21'-4" X 21'-8"

WALK

DRIVEWAY

34'-0"

FIRST FLOOR
No. 20055

BEDROOM 3
11'-4" X 11'-6"

B.

LIVING ROOM BELOW

DN.

H.

C.

L.

S.L.

BEDROOM 2
11'-0" X 11'-4"

C.

DRESSING AREA

B.

LIN.

C.

SLOPE   SLOPE

SEAT

M. BEDROOM
14'-8" X 11'-4"

SECOND FLOOR

Total living area — 1,701 sq. ft.

For Year-Round Recreational Use

No. 91725

This cabin designed for year-round recreational use has a long sun porch, complete with sink, stretching across most of the back of the cabin. When temperatures climb into the comfort zone and beyond, a wide deck nearly doubles the available living area. The sturdy woodstove pumps out enough heat to keep the cabin cozy. The kitchen is surprisingly large and seems even larger because it is completely open to the lofty dining and living room. The first floor bathroom is compartmentalized, with the toilet and and oversize shower separate from the lavatory. Access is from two sides — through the utility room, or the living room. Upstairs, a bathroom with a tub, serves the two narrow bedrooms. A large linen closet fills the space in front of the stairs, at the landing.

First floor — 1,040 sq. ft.
Second floor — 383 sq. ft.

Total living area — 1,423 sq. ft.

No. 91725

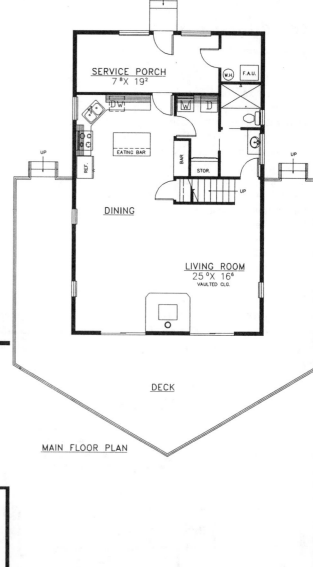

MAIN FLOOR PLAN

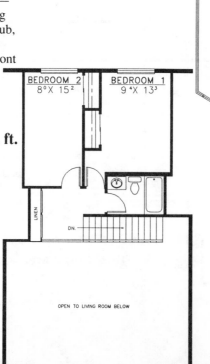

UPPER LEVEL PLAN

Suited for a Hill

No. 90822

Use this compact A-frame year round or as a vacation retreat. Either way, this practical design is bound to give you pleasure for a long, long time. The main floor, with its vaulted ceilings and fieldstone fireplace, combines kitchen, living and dining rooms with two bedrooms and a full bath. The wrap-around sundeck affords lots of outdoor living space. With its soaring views of the floor below, the loft contains the master suite and the perfect place for a home office.

Main floor area — 925 sq. ft.
Loft — 338 sq. ft.
Basement — 864 sq. ft.
Width — 33'-0"
Depth — 47'-0"

Total living area — 1,263 sq. ft.

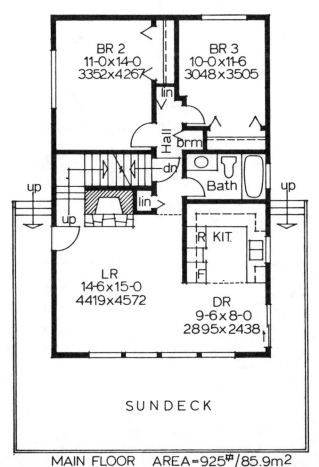

MAIN FLOOR   AREA=925#/85.9m2

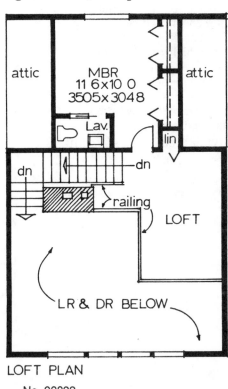

LOFT PLAN
No. 90822

Privacy Zones

No. 91506

Do you want one-level living without compromising your privacy? Here's a home that will house your family in easy-care elegance, with bedrooms tucked away from the bustle of active areas. The central foyer opens to a large living and dining room combination brightened by a sun-catching bay window. At the rear of the house, an open plan allows the fireplace in the family room to spread its warmth through the angular, efficient kitchen and cheerful nook with sliders to the rear patio. A hallway off the foyer leads to the three bedrooms, laundry room, and handy garage entry. A hall bath serves the kids' rooms, but the master suite features its own private bath with step-in shower.

Main living area — 1,546 sq. ft.
Garage — 2-car

Total living area — 1,546 sq. ft.

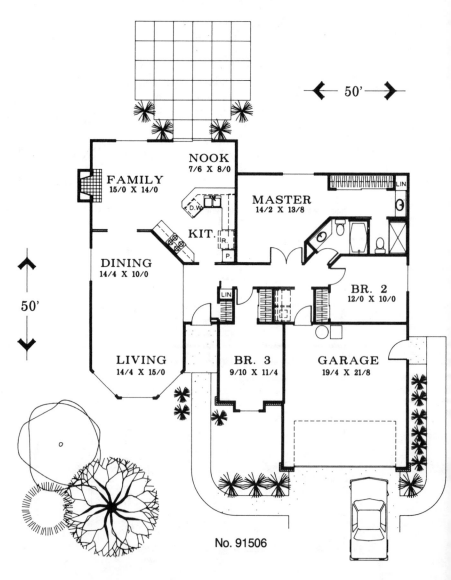

No. 91506

Comfortable Family Room in Congenial Setting

No. 90520

A secluded porch provides an intimate entrance to this 3 bedroom home. You'll appreciate the large family room with fireplace as the center for many activities. The breakfast nook will be popular with its nearby bow window and will be practical near the pantry and kitchen. The dining area, also, is easy to serve. The living room will have a wonderful view through the bow window. The master bedroom is complete, including dressing area and walk-in wardrobe.

First floor — 1,048 sq. ft.
Second floor — 726 sq. ft.
Garage — 2-car

Total living area — 1,774 sq. ft.

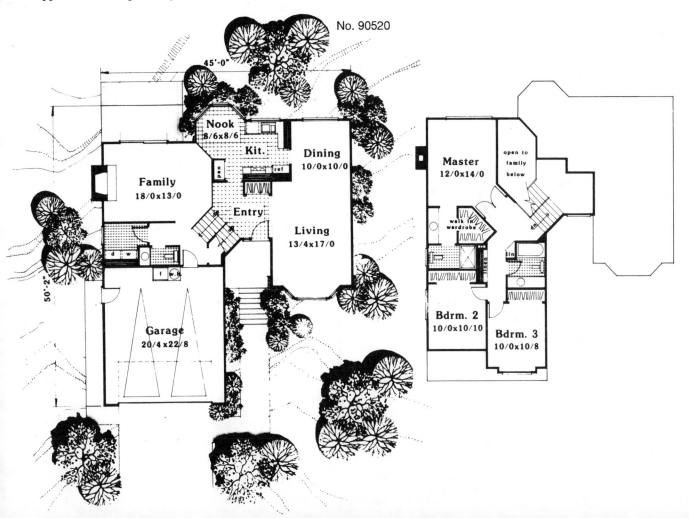

No. 90520

45'-0"

50'-2"

Nook
8/6x8/6

Kit.

Dining
10/0x10/0

ref

Family
18/0x13/0

cap

Entry

Living
13/4x17/0

d w

Garage
20/4 x 22/8

Master
12/0x14/0

open to
family
below

walk in
wardrobe

Bdrm. 2
10/0x10/10

Bdrm. 3
10/0x10/8

No Wasted Space

No. 90412

The open floor plan of this modified A-frame design virtually eliminates wasted hall space. The centrally located Great room features a cathedral ceiling with exposed wood beams and large areas of fixed glass on both front and rear. Living and dining areas are virtually separated by a massive stone fireplace. The isolated master suite features a walk-in closet and sliding

glass doors opening onto the front deck. A walk-thru utility room provides easy access from the carport and outside storage areas to the compact kitchen. On the opposite side of the Great room are two additional bedrooms and a second full bath. A full length deck and vertical wood siding with stone accents on the corners provide a rustic yet contemporary

exterior. Specify crawlspace, basement or slab foundation when ordering.

Main living area — 1,454 sq. ft.

Total living area — 1,454 sq. ft.

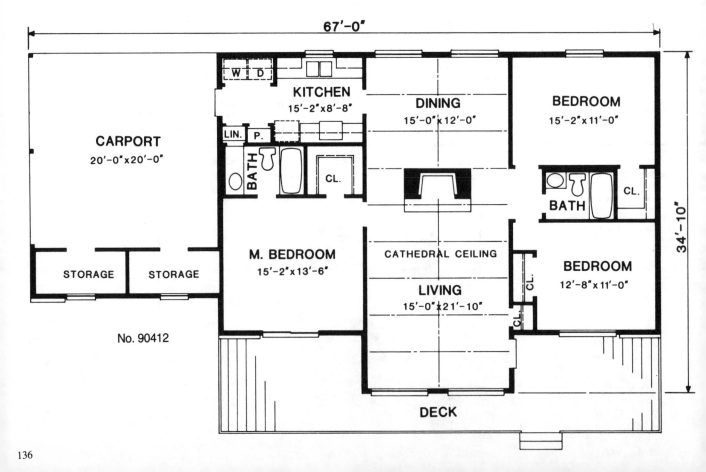

Soaring Ceilings Add Space and Drama

No. 90288

Here's a one-level home with an airy feeling accentuated by oversized windows and well-placed skylights. You'll love the attractive garden court that adds privacy to the front facing bedroom, the sheltered porch that opens to a central foyer, and the wide-open active areas. Two bedrooms, tucked down a hall off the foyer, include the sunny master suite with its sloping ceilings, private terrace entry, and luxurious garden bath with adjoining dressing room. The gathering room, study, and formal dining room flow together along the rear of the house, sharing the warmth of the gathering room fireplace, and a magnificent view of the terrace. Convenient pass-throughs add to the efficiency of the galley kitchen and adjoining breakfast room.

Main living area — 1,387 sq. ft.
Garage — 440 sq. ft.

Total living area — 1,387 sq. ft.

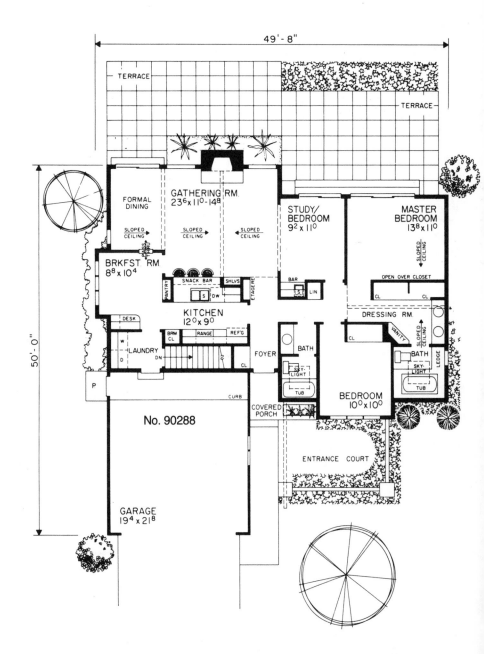

Country Living in a Doll House

No. 90410

Front porch, dormers, shutters and a bay window on the exterior of this rustic design are complemented by an informal interior. The main floor is divided into three sections. The eat-in country kitchen with island counter and bay window and a large utility room which can be entered from either the kitchen or garage. The second section is the Great room with fireplace, an informal dining nook and double doors opening onto the rear deck or screened-in porch. The master suite features a walk-in closet and compartmentalized bath. The second floor consists of a full bath, two bedrooms and a large storage room. This plan is available with a basement or crawlspace foundation. Please specify when ordering.

First floor — 1,277 sq. ft.
Second floor — 720 sq. ft.
Garage — 2-car

Total living area — 1,997 sq. ft.

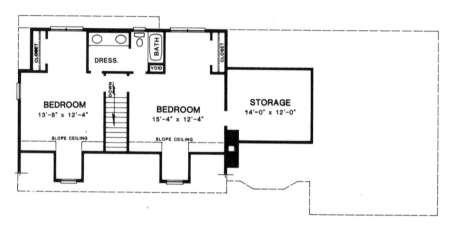

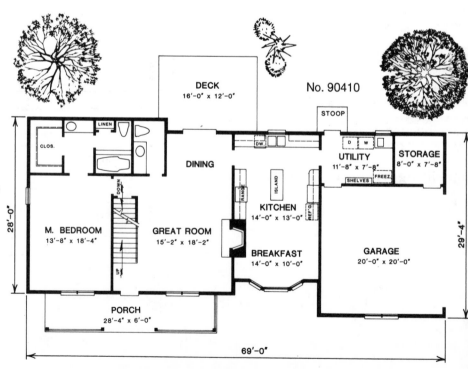

A *Touch of Classic Elegance*

No. 20079

There's no wasted space in this compact home that combines the best of classic design and modern convenience. If you're a traditionalist, you'll love the half-round windows, clapboard and brick facade, and cozy fireplace. But, from the moment you walk past the portico, you'll find exciting contemporary touches: soaring ceilings, a dramatic balcony, a U-shaped kitchen, and wide-open living areas. Laundry facilities are conveniently adjacent to downstairs bedrooms. You'll enjoy retreating upstairs to your very private master suite.

First floor — 1,200 sq. ft.
Second floor — 461 sq. ft.
Garage — 475 sq. ft.
Basement — 1,200 sq. ft.

Total living area — 1,661 sq. ft.

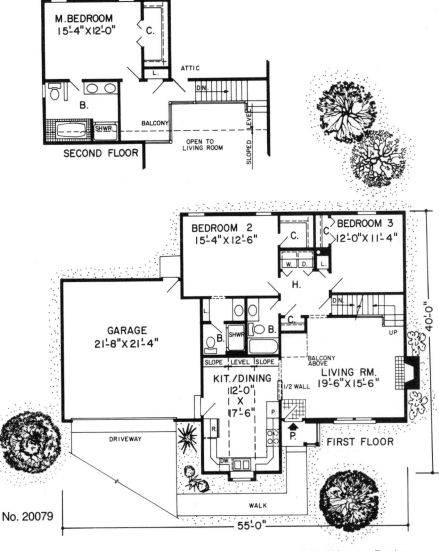

No. 20079

A Karl Kreeger Design

Your Classic Hideaway

No. 90423

Don't limit this design. Such a tranquil plan could maximize a vacation or suit retirement, as well as be a wonderful family home. It's large enough to welcome a crowd, but small enough for easy upkeep. The only stairs go to the basement. The lavish master suite, with its sunken tub, melts away cares. Either guest bedroom is big enough for two. The lovely fireplace is both cozy and a source of heat for the core area of the home. Note how the country kitchen connects to the large dining and living space. With a screened porch, laundry alcove, and large garage for storage, you'll have everything you need with a minimum of maintenance and cleaning. Specify basement, crawlspace, or slab foundation.

Main living area — 1,773 sq. ft.
Screened porch — 240 sq. ft.
Garage — 2-car

Total living area — 1,773 sq. ft.

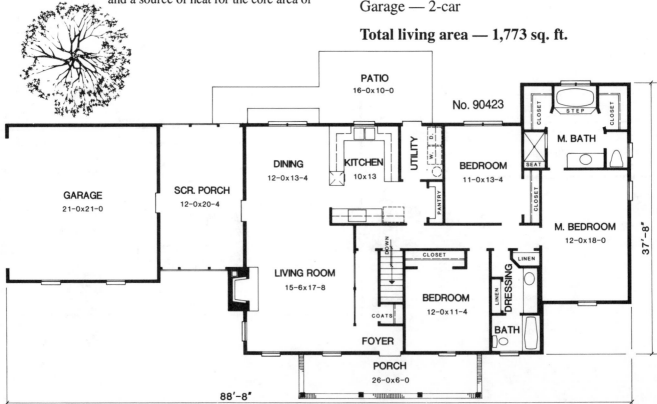

Rustic Warmth

No. 90440

While the covered porch and huge, fieldstone fireplace lend a rustic air to this three-bedroom classic, the interior is loaded with the amenities you've been seeking. Doesn't a book-lined, fireplaced living room sound nice? Haven't you been longing for a fully-equipped island kitchen? This one adjoins a sunny dining room with sliders to a wood deck. Does the idea of a first-floor master suite just steps away from your morning coffee sound

good? Tucked upstairs with another full bath, two bedrooms feature walk-in closets and cozy, sloping ceilings. There's even plenty of extra storage space in the attic.

First floor — 1,100 sq. ft.
Second floor — 664 sq. ft.
Basement — 1,100 sq. ft.
Garage — 2-car

Total living area — 1,764 sq. ft.

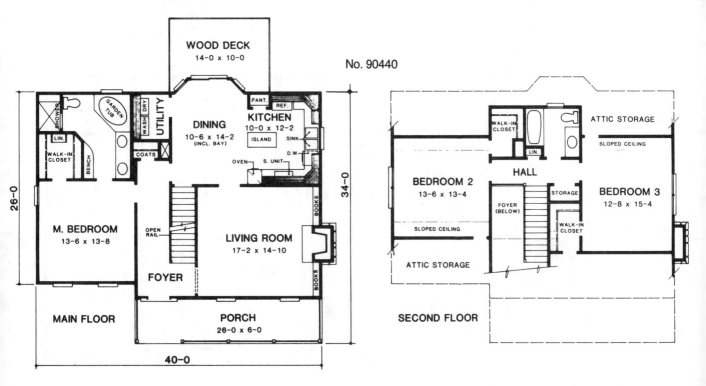

Living Areas Warmed by Massive Fireplace

No. 10752

Here's a handsome home for the family that enjoys one-level living. Skylights, sloping ceilings, and an absence of walls give active areas an irresistable, spacious atmosphere. And, with a floor-to-ceiling window wall in the living room and French doors in the dining room, interior spaces enjoy a pleasing unity with the great outdoors. Whether you're in the mood for formal or informal dining, the centrally located kitchen will make mealtime a breeze. Three bedrooms, each featuring a walk-in closet, occupy their own quiet wing off the foyer. The front bedrooms share a full bath with double vanities. The master suite at the rear of the house enjoys a private bath.

Main living area — 1,890 sq. ft.
Garage — 488 sq. ft.

Total living area — 1,890 sq. ft.

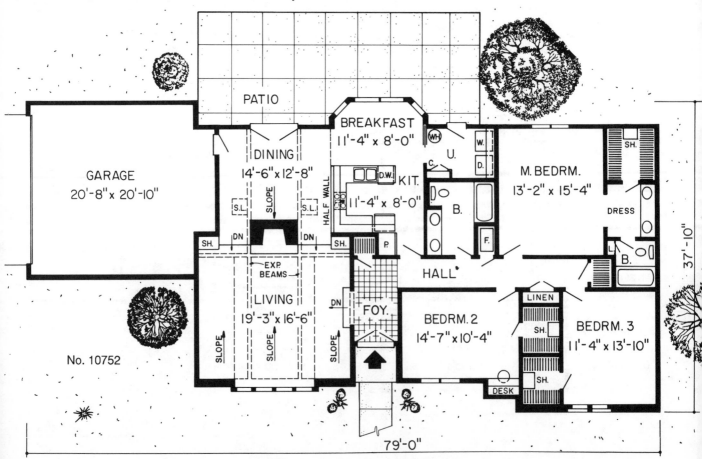

Foyer Isolates Bedroom Wing

No. 20087

Don't worry about waking up the kids. They'll sleep soundly in a quiet atmosphere away from main living areas, on a hallway off the foyer of this charming one-level. Sunny and open, the living room features a window-wall flanking a massive fireplace, and access to a deck at the rear of the house. The adjoining dining room boasts recessed ceilings, and pass-through convenience to the kitchen and breakfast room. You'll find the master suite, tucked behind the two-car garage for maximum quiet, a pleasant retreat that includes double vanities, a walk-in closet, and both shower and tub.

Main living area — 1,568 sq. ft.
Basement — 1,568 sq. ft.
Garage — 484 sq. ft.

Total living area — 1,568 sq. ft.

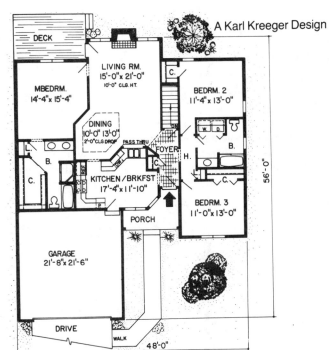

No. 20087

A Karl Kreeger Design

DECK

LIVING RM.
15'-0" x 21'-0"
10'-0" CLG. HT.

MBEDRM.
14'-4" x 15'-4"

BEDRM. 2
11'-4" x 13'-0"

DINING
10'-0" 13'-0"
2'-0" CLG DROP

PASS THRU

FOYER

KITCHEN/BRKFST
17'-4" x 11'-10"

BEDRM. 3
11'-0" x 13'-0"

PORCH

GARAGE
21'-8" x 21'-6"

DRIVE

WALK

48'-0"

56'-0"

Fireplace Adds a Cozy Touch

No. 10760

Here's a handsome split-entry home that separates active and quiet areas. Step down to the garage level that includes a basement recreation and workshop area perfect for the household hobbyist. A short staircase leads up to the soaring living room, where the open feeling is accentuated by a huge bow window and a wide opening to the formal dining room. The kitchen lies behind swinging double doors, and features access to a raised rear deck. A few steps up, you'll find two full baths and three bedrooms with extra-large closets. Sloped-ceilings add dramatic appeal to the private bedroom wing.

First floor — 1,676 sq. ft.
Basement recreation area —
    592 sq. ft.
Workshop — 144 sq. ft.
Garage — 697 sq. ft.

Total living area — 1,676 sq. ft.

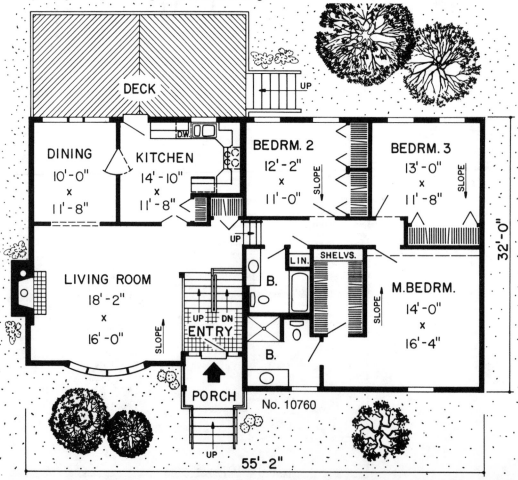

No. 10760

Traditional Elements Combine in Friendly Colonial

No. 90606

Casual living is the theme of this elegant Farmhouse Colonial. A beautiful circular stair ascends from the central foyer, flanked by the formal living and dining rooms. The informal family room, accessible from the foyer, captures the Early American style with exposed beams, wood paneling, and brick fireplace wall. A separate dinette opens to an efficient kitchen. Four bedrooms and a two-basin family bath, arranged around the central hall, occupy the second floor.

First floor — 1,023 sq. ft.
Second floor — 923 sq. ft.
Garage — 2-car
(optional slab construction available)

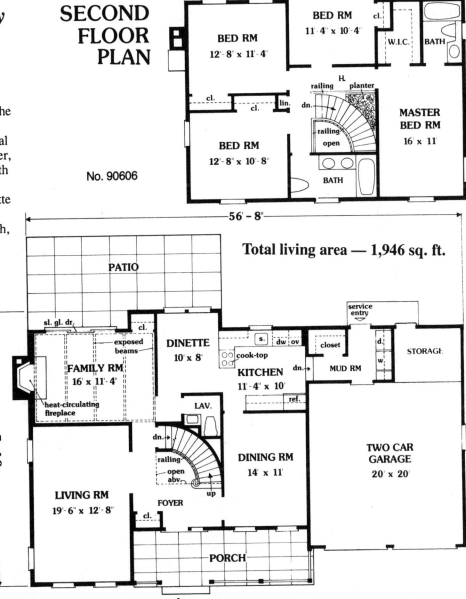

SECOND FLOOR PLAN

No. 90606

2x6 studs for added insulation

BED RM 12'-8" x 11'-4"

BED RM 11'-4" x 10'-4"

W.I.C.

BATH

cl.

cl.

lin.

dn.

railing planter

railing open

MASTER BED RM 16' x 11'

BED RM 12'-8" x 10'-8"

BATH

Total living area — 1,946 sq. ft.

56'-8"

34'-2"

PATIO

sl. gl. dr.

cl.

exposed beams

FAMILY RM 16' x 11'-4"

heat-circulating fireplace

DINETTE 10' x 8'

s.

cook-top

dw ov

KITCHEN 11'-4" x 10'

ref.

service entry

closet

MUD RM

dn.

d. w

STORAGE

LAV.

dn.

railing open abv.

up

DINING RM 14' x 11'

TWO CAR GARAGE 20' x 20'

LIVING RM 19'-6" x 12'-8"

FOYER

cl.

PORCH

FIRST FLOOR PLAN

Compact and Appealing

No. 20075

Here's an L-shaped country charmer with a porch that demands a rocking chair or two. You'll appreciate the convenient one-level design that separates active and sleeping areas. Right off the foyer, the formal dining and living rooms have a wide-open feeling, thanks to extra wide doorways and a recessed ceiling. The kitchen is centrally located for maximum convenience. For informal family meals, you'll delight in the sunny breakfast nook that links the fireplaced living room and outdoor deck. Enjoy those quiet hours in the three bedrooms separated from family living spaces. With its own double-sink full bath and walk-in closet, the master suite will be your favorite retreat.

Main living area — 1,682 sq. ft.
Basement — 1,682 sq. ft.
Garage — 484 sq. ft.

Total living area — 1,682 sq. ft.

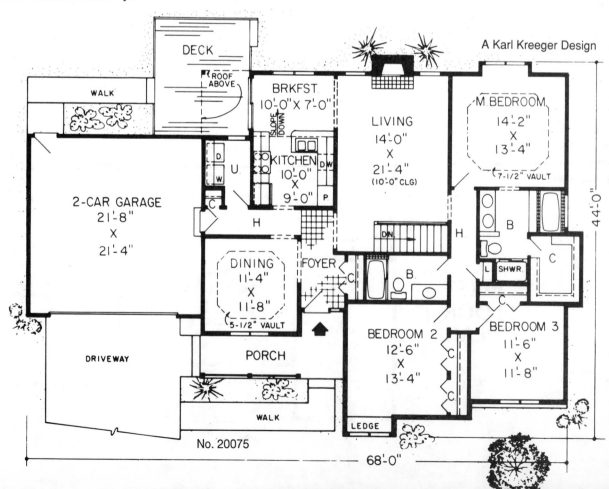

Multiple Peaks Add Interesting Angles

No. 10600

This Tudor style 3-bedroom home is unusually attractive with its stone accents and impressive windows. Its useable rooms appear larger thanks to sloped ceilings and a tasteful floor plan. A quaint breakfast nook with bow window provides a buffer between the no-nonsense kitchen and elegant, airy dining room. Comfort comes naturally in the living room which features a large fireplace with stone hearth. An outside patio is easily accessible through sliding doors and enjoys private access to the master bedroom.

Main living area — 1,219 sq. ft.
Garage — 410 sq. ft.

Total living area — 1,219 sq. ft.

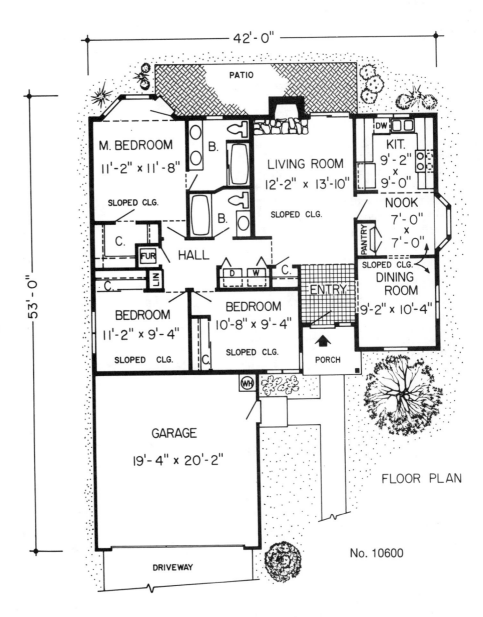

FLOOR PLAN

No. 10600

Designed for Family Living

No. 90604

The grand, circular staircase will charm your guests as they enter this traditional three-bedroom loaded with family features. Flanked by formal dining and living rooms, the foyer leads straight into the family living area of the house, with utility room entry for muddy kids and grocery-laden parents. The cozy family room with raised hearth is a comfortable center for group activities. Four bedrooms, two baths, and closets galore make this a house you can enjoy for many, happy years.

First floor — 952 sq. ft.
Second floor — 892 sq. ft.
(excluding garage, laundry, storage)

Total living area — 1,844 sq. ft.

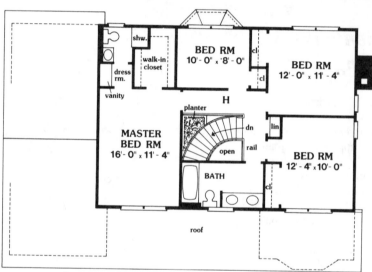

SECOND FLOOR PLAN

No. 90604

FIRST FLOOR PLAN

Tradition with a Twist

No. 90933

A traditional exterior hides a multitude of special features that distinguish this attractive four-bedroom abode. The inviting porch leads into the central foyer, illuminated by a skylight far overhead. You'll find the living and formal dining rooms adjacent to the entry, with informal family areas grouped conveniently at the rear of the house. Separated from the breakfast nook only by a railing, the sunken family room is warmed by a fireplace. Upstairs, the master suite boasts an added attraction — a hidden sundeck, tucked behind the garage for privacy.

First floor — 1,104 sq. ft.

Second floor — 845 sq. ft.

Garage & workshop — 538 sq. ft.

Unfinished basement — 1,098 sq. ft.

Width — 55 ft.

Depth — 32 ft.

Total living area — 1,949 sq. ft.

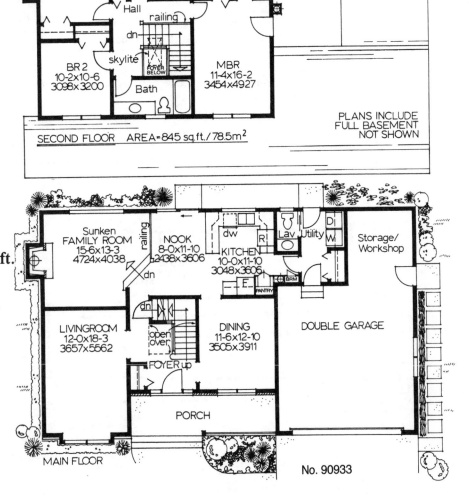

SECOND FLOOR   AREA=845 sq.ft./78.5m²

PLANS INCLUDE
FULL BASEMENT
NOT SHOWN

MAIN FLOOR

No. 90933

Mud Room Separates Garage and Kitchen

No. 9812

Gardening and woodworking tools will find a home in the storage closet of the useful mudroom in this rustic detailed ranch. Besides incorporating a laundry area, the mudroom will prove invaluable as a place for removing snowy boots and draining wet umbrellas. The family room appendages the open kitchen and flows outward to the stone terrace. The master bedroom is furnished with a private bath and protruding closet space, and the living room retains a formality by being situated to the left of the entryway.

First floor — 1,396 sq. ft.
Basement — 1,396 sq. ft.
Garage — 484 sq. ft.

Total living area — 1,396 sq. ft.

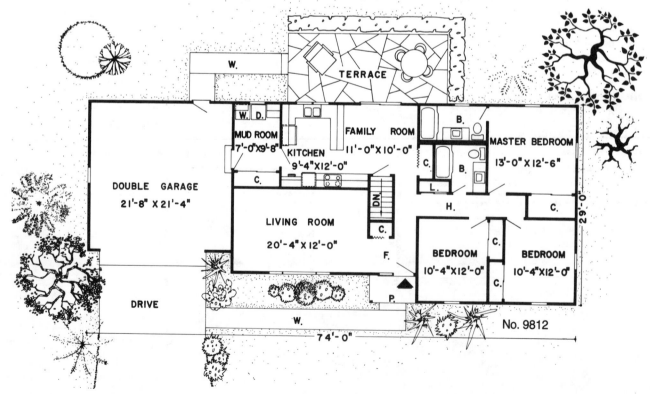

Expansive, Not Expensive

No. 90623

Despite its compact area, this home looks and lives like a luxurious ranch. A decorative screen divides the entrance foyer from the spacious, comfortable living room, which flows into the pleasant dining room overlooking a rear garden. The roomy, eat-in kitchen features a planning corner. And, the adjacent laundry-mudroom provides access to the two-car garage and to the outdoors. Here also lie the stairs to the full basement, a valuable, functional part of the house which adds many possibilities for informal family living. The private bedroom wing includes three bedrooms and two baths.

Total living area — 1,370 sq. ft.

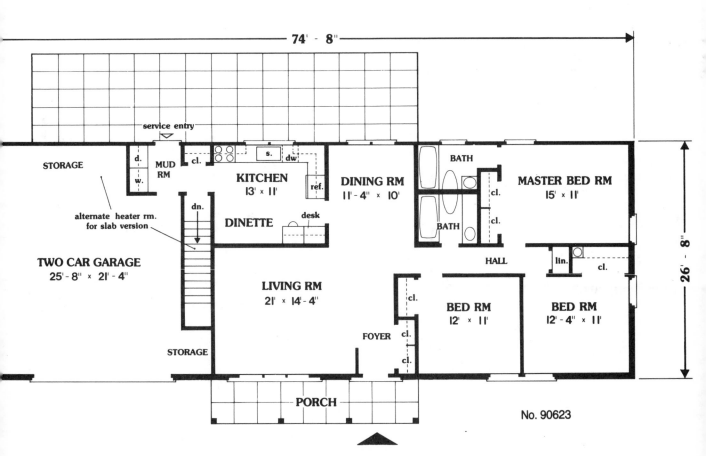

No. 90623

Inexpensive Ranch Design

No. 20062

This simple but inexpensive ranch design has a brick and vertical siding exterior. The interior has a well set-up kitchen area with its own breakfast area by a large picture window. A formal dining room is located near the kitchen. The living room has one open beam across a sloping ceiling. A large hearth is in front of a wood burning fireplace. Inside the front entrance a tiled foyer incorporates closet space and has many different room entrances through which an individual can walk. Three bedrooms are offered in this design. The master bedroom has an extremely large bath area with its own walk-in closet. Two other bedrooms share a full bath. There is also a linen closet and a closet for the washer and dryer area. A two-car garage is offered in this plan.

Main floor — 1,500 sq. ft.
Basement — 1,500 sq. ft.
Garage — 482 sq. ft.

Total living area — 1,500 sq. ft.

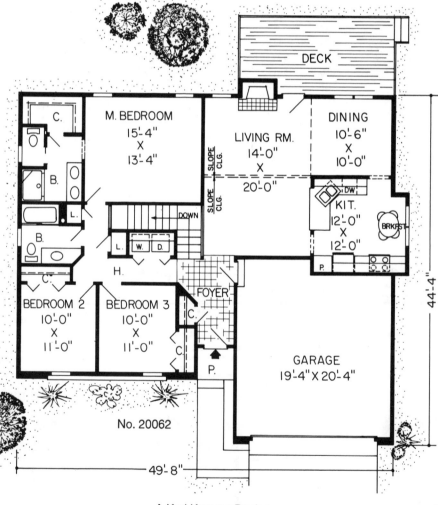

A Karl Kreeger Design

For The Young At Heart

No. 99324

For the move-down buyers on the go or the family on the grow, this three bedroom home has all the right features. The home draws its look from the nostalgic elements of older traditional homes. It has half-round transom and gable details, divided light windows, covered entry porch and bay windows. The interior features a vaulted Great room with fireplace and transom window, and a vaulted kitchen with breakfast area and sliders to the deck. The master suite has its own bath.

Main living area — 1,307 sq. ft.
Garage — 2-car

Total living area — 1,307 sq. ft

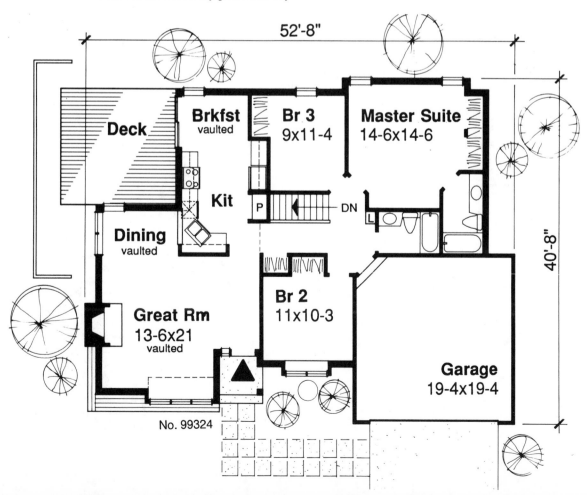

52'-8"

40'-8"

Deck

Brkfst vaulted

Br 3 9x11-4

Master Suite 14-6x14-6

Kit

P DN L

Dining vaulted

Great Rm 13-6x21 vaulted

Br 2 11x10-3

Garage 19-4x19-4

No. 99324

Compact Victorian Ideal for Narrow Lot

No. 90406

This compact Victorian design incorporates four bedrooms and three full baths into a 30 foot wide home. The upstairs master suite features two closets, an oversized tub, and a sitting room with vaulted ceiling and bay window. Two additional bedrooms and a second full bath are included in the upper level. A fourth bedroom and third full bath on the main floor can serve as an in-law or guest suite. Between the dining and breakfast rooms is a galley kitchen. The dining room has a bay window and the breakfast room a utility nook. A large parlor with a raised-hearth fireplace completes the main floor. The porches add to the overall exterior appearances and help to protect the front and side entrances. This plan is available with a crawlspace or basement foundation, please specify when ordering. Also please specify elevation A or B.

First floor — 954 sq. ft.
Second floor — 783 sq. ft.

Total living area — 1,737 sq. ft.

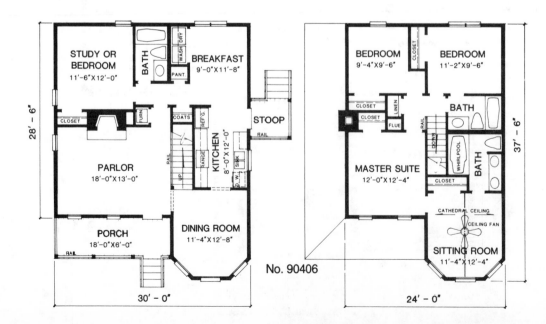

Victorian Touches Disguise Modern Design

No. 90616

Indulge the romance of Victorian styling without sacrificing up-to-date living. Out of the past come porches with turned wood posts, exterior walls of round shingles, wonderful bay windows, and decorative scroll work. But the present is evident in the kitchen and family room, with a skylighted entertainment area for today's electronic pleasures. The stair begins its rise with a turned post and rail. The master suite features a high ceiling with an arched window, private bath, and tower sitting room with adjoining roof deck. Basement and crawspace foundation options included with this plan

Main living area — 1,956 sq. ft.
Laundry — 36 sq. ft.
Basement — 967 sq. ft.
Garage — 440 sq. ft.

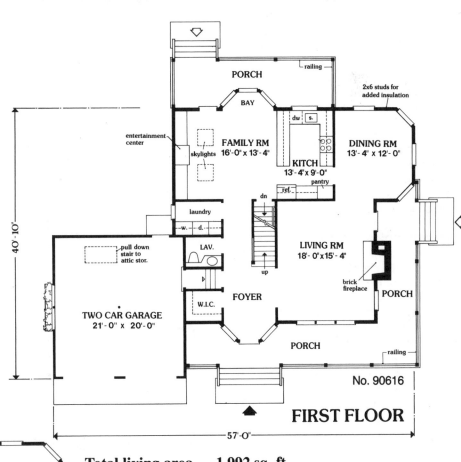

Total living area — 1,992 sq. ft.

No. 90616

FIRST FLOOR

PORCH
BAY
entertainment center
skylights
FAMILY RM
16'-0" x 13'-4"
DINING RM
13'-4" x 12'-0"
2x6 studs for added insulation
KITCH
13'-4" x 9'-0"
dw s.
ref.
pantry
dn
laundry
w. d.
LAV.
LIVING RM
18'-0" x 15'-4"
up
brick fireplace
PORCH
pull down stair to attic stor.
W.I.C.
FOYER
TWO CAR GARAGE
21'-0" x 20'-0"
PORCH
railing
40'-0"
57'-0"

SECOND FLOOR

BED RM
11'-0" x 10'-0"
BATH
BED RM
13'-4" x 11'-0"
cl
lin
dn
stor.
cl
H
BATH
lin
railing
DECK
W.I.C.
MASTER SUITE
15'-4" x 12'-8"
high ceiling
railing
TOWER

Open Spaces

No. 91505

This spacious home achieves a wonderful, sun-washed atmosphere through intelligent space planning, generous windows, and vaulted ceilings. An angular, open staircase divides the two-story foyer from the vaulted living and dining rooms. A dramatic den just off the foyer features a window wall overlooking the street. And the informal area at the rear of the house is one huge expanse separated by a handy work island in the kitchen and high ceilings in the fireplaced family room. Enjoy the view from the balcony at the top of the stairs that links three bedrooms and two baths. In the master suite, vaulted ceilings, a skylit bath, and garden spa behind a glass-block wall continue the wide-open atmosphere.

First floor — 1,152 sq. ft.
Second floor — 823 sq. ft.
Garage — 2-car

Total living area — 1,975 sq. ft.

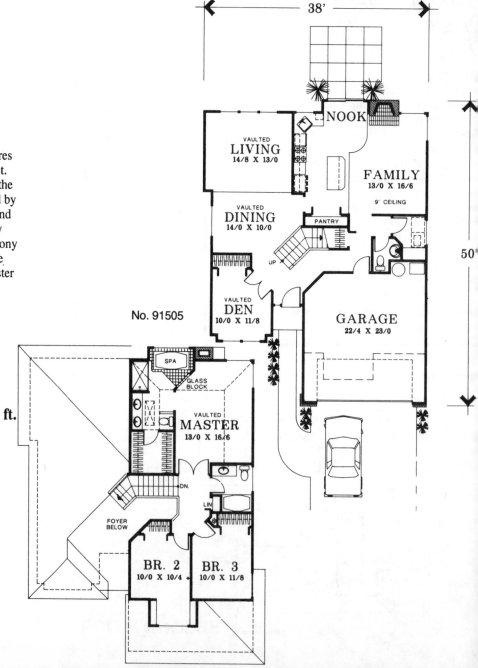

No. 91505

unny Breakfast Bay

o. 91352

is compact three bedroom house fits
cely on a 50 ft. wide lot. The hipped
f and exterior courtyard create an
pearance of a much larger house than
e 1,288 sq. ft. it contains. Formal and
sual dining areas are both provided
th the breakfast room opening to a
all patio. The fenced and gated
urtyard maintains privacy for
nning or outside dining. Angled
lls through the interior provide
eresting traffic patterns. Built-in
ina closets add to the ambiance of
s home plan.

ain living area — 1,288 sq. ft.
arage — 2-car

otal living area — 1,288 sq. ft.

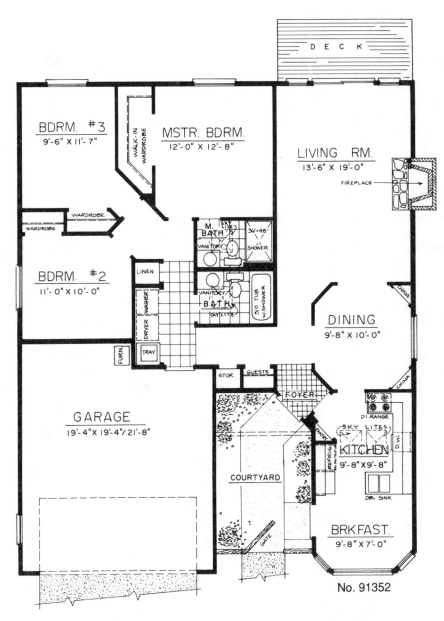

No. 91352

Built-In Beauty

No. 91507

From its skylit foyer to the garden spa in the master suite, this carefree home possesses a sunny charm you'll love coming home to. The living room features a bump-out window that enhances its wide-open arrangement with the formal dining room. At the rear of the house, the efficient island kitchen combines with a cheerful dining nook and fireplaced family room for a spacious, comfortable area just perfect for informal get-togethers. Down a short hall off the foyer, two bedrooms and a full bath flank the laundry room and handy garage entry. The master suite lies behind elegant double doors, boasting a luxurious, private bath with every amenity.

Main living area — 1,687 sq. ft.
Garage — 2-car

Total living area — 1,687 sq. ft.

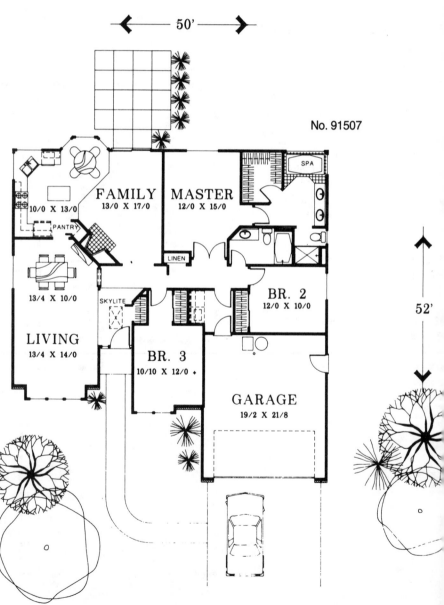

50'

No. 91507

FAMILY
13/0 X 17/0

MASTER
12/0 X 15/0

SPA

10/0 X 13/0

PANTRY

LINEN

13/4 X 10/0

BR. 2
12/0 X 10/0

SKYLITE

LIVING
13/4 X 14/0

BR. 3
10/10 X 12/0

GARAGE
19/2 X 21/8

52'

Formal Balance

No. 91502

This elegant home offers all the features demanded by today's busy family in a classic package. Look at the magnificent two-story foyer crowned by a towering palladium window, the special detailing under the eaves, and the traditional clapboard exterior adorned with a brick chimney. Inside, the foyer is flanked by the formal living room and the cozy family room with brick hearth. At mealtime, choose between the formal dining room that adjoins the living room, the sunny nook off the angular kitchen, or the patio just outside. Upstairs, three bedrooms include a magnificent master suite with garden spa and double vanities. And the bonus room provides plenty of room for growth.

First floor — 935 sq. ft.
Second floor — 772 sq. ft.
Bonus room — 177 sq. ft.
Garage — 2-car

Total living area — 1,884 sq. ft.

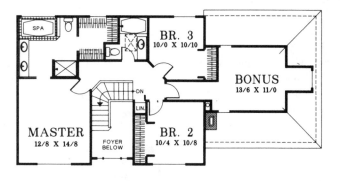

No. 91502

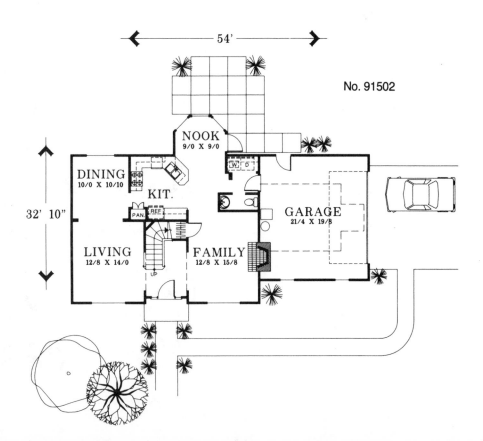

No. 91502

Compact Home for a Small Space

No. 90500

A massive bay window is the dominant feature in the facade of this cozy home with attached two-car garage. From the entry, there are three ways to walk. Turn left into the fireplaced living room and adjoining dining room. Or walk straight into the kitchen and breakfast nook, which extends to a covered porch. Step down the hall on the right to the master suite, full bath, and a second bedroom. The TV room, which can double as a third bedroom, completes the circular floor plan in this convenient, one-level abode.

Main living area — 1,299 sq. ft.
Garage — 2-car

Total living area — 1,299 sq. ft.

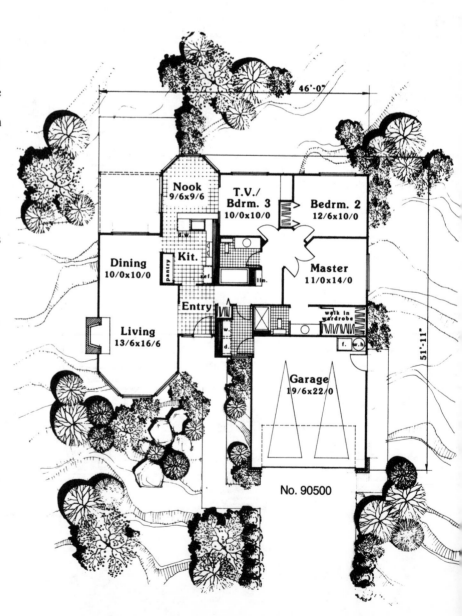

No. 90500

Carefree Comfort

No. 91418

Easy living awaits you in this one-level traditional designed with privacy in mind. A dramatic, vaulted-foyer separates active areas from the three bedrooms. Down the skylit hall lies the master suite, where you'll discover the luxury of a private patio off the book-lined reading nook, decorative ceilings, and a well-appointed bath. The soaring roof line of the foyer continues into the Great room, which combines with the bayed dining room to create a celebration of open space enhanced by abundant windows. The cook in the house will love the rangetop island kitchen and nook arrangement, loaded with storage inside, and surrounded by a built-in planter outside that's perfect for an herb garden.

Main living area — 1,665 sq. ft.
Garage — 2-car

Total living area — 1,665 sq. ft.

ALTERNATE BASEMENT PLAN

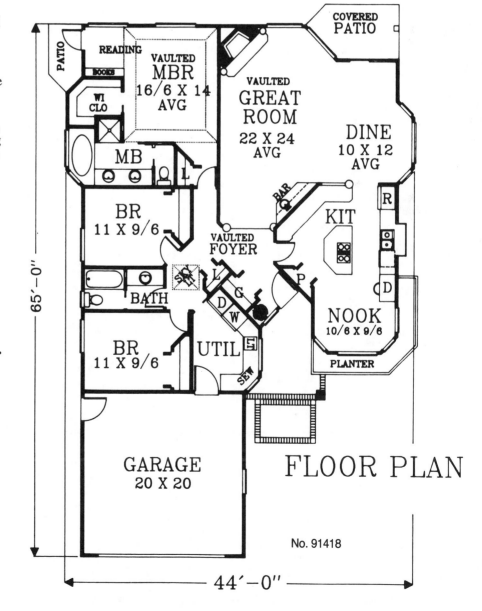

FLOOR PLAN

No. 91418

Delightful Doll House

No. 20161

With its railed porch and gingerbread trim, this convenient ranch looks like a Victorian doll house. But there's lots of room in this compact, three-bedroom plan. The foyer, tucked between the two-car garage and bedroom wing, opens to a spacious, fireplaced living room. Soaring ceilings and an open arrangement with the adjoining dining room add to the airy feeling in this sunny space. The kitchen, steps away, offers easy, over-the-counter service at mealtime. And there's a large pantry just across from the adjacent laundry room. The two front bedrooms share a full bath. The master suite boasts its own private bath, plus a closet-lined wall and decorative touches that make it special.

Basement — 1,298 sq. ft.
Garage — 462 sq. ft.

Total living area — 1,307 sq. ft.

No. 20161

A Karl Kreeger Design

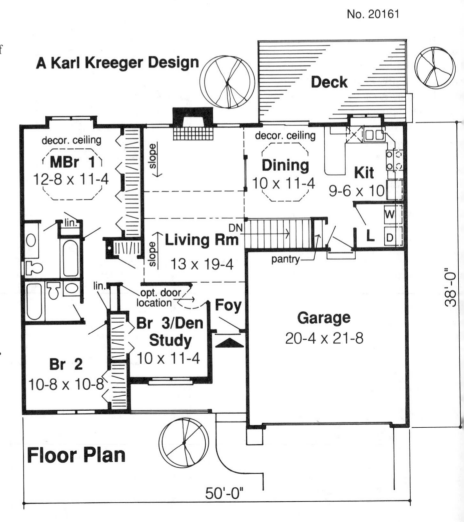

Deck

decor. ceiling
MBr 1
12-8 x 11-4

slope

decor. ceiling
Dining
10 x 11-4

Kit
9-6 x 10

lin.

slope

Living Rm
13 x 19-4

DN

pantry

W
L
D

lin.

opt. door
location

Foy

**Br 3/Den
Study**
10 x 11-4

Garage
20-4 x 21-8

Br 2
10-8 x 10-8

Floor Plan

38'-0"

50'-0"

162

Cathedral Window Graced by Massive Arch

No. 20066

A tiled threshold provides a distinctive entrance into this spacious home. There's room for gracious living everywhere, from the comfortable living room with a wood-burning fireplace and tiled hearth, to the elegant dining room with a vaulted-ceiling, to the outside deck. Plan your meals in a kitchen that has all the right ingredients: a central work island, pantry, planning desk, and breakfast area. A decorative ceiling will delight your eye in the master suite, which includes a full bath and bow window.

Main living area — 1,850 sq. ft.
Basement — 1,850 sq. ft.
Garage — 503 sq. ft.

Total living area — 1,850 sq. ft.

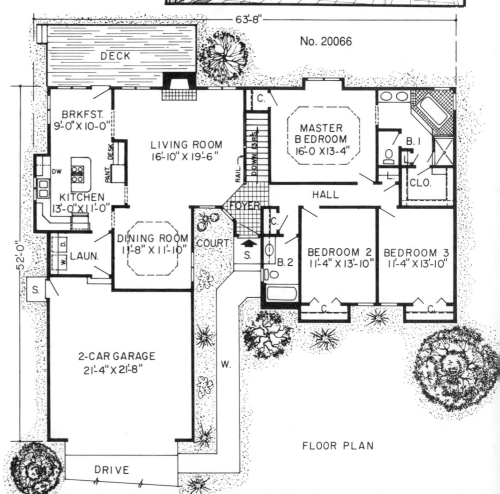

FLOOR PLAN

Country Classic Full of Character

No. 90397

Towering gables softened by gentle arches add old-fashioned charm to this tidy, three-bedroom traditional. But look at the updated interior. Corner transom windows create a sunny atmosphere throughout the open plan. A fireplace divides the vaulted living room and dining room, contributing to the spacious, yet warm feeling in this inviting home. Any cook would envy the efficient layout of the country kitchen, with its corner sink overlooking the deck and family sitting area. Even your plants will enjoy the greenhouse atmosphere of the vaulted master suite, which features a double-vanitied bath and walk-in closet. Another full bath serves the children's rooms.

First floor — 834 sq. ft.
Second floor — 722 sq. ft.
Garage — 2-car

Total living area — 1556 sq. ft.

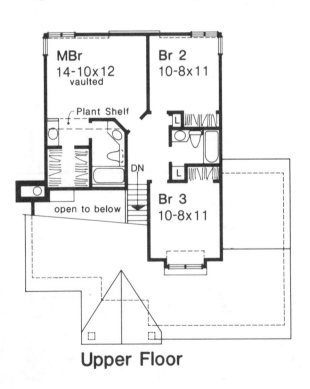

Upper Floor

MBr
14-10x12
vaulted

Plant Shelf

Br 2
10-8x11

open to below

DN

Br 3
10-8x11

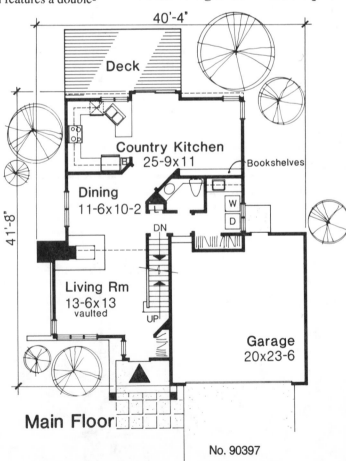

Main Floor

40'-4"

Deck

Country Kitchen
25-9x11

Bookshelves

Dining
11-6x10-2

41'-8"

W
D

Living Rm
13-6x13
vaulted

DN

UP

Garage
20x23-6

No. 90397

Luxurious Master Suite

No. 90329

On the second floor, the roomy master bedroom with its luxurious master bath and dressing area will be a constant delight. Just a step down from the bedroom itself, the bath incorporates an oversized corner tub, a shower, a walk-in closet, and a skylight. The third bedroom could serve as a loft or sitting room. The open staircase spirals down to the first floor Great room with its vaulted ceiling, fireplace, and corner of windows. The adjacent dining room has a wetbar and direct access to the large, eat-in kitchen. Additional living space is provided by the family room which opens onto the deck through sliding glass doors.

Main floor — 904 sq. ft.
Upper floor — 797 sq. ft.
Basement — 904 sq. ft.
Garage — 405 sq. ft.

Total living area — 1,701 sq. ft.

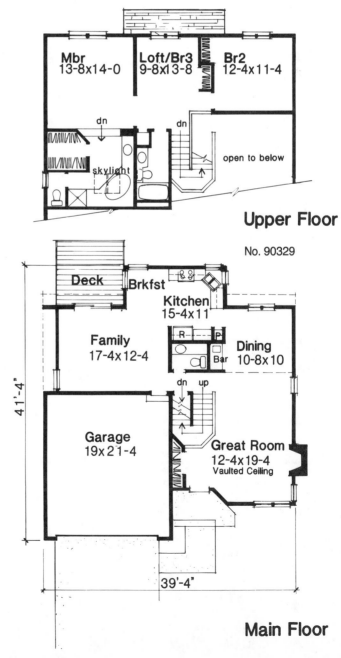

Open Floor Plan Enhanced by Sloped Ceilings

No. 90125

A step down from the tiled entrance area, guests may overlook an expansive living area composed of the Great room and the dining room. Warmed by a fireplace and further enhanced by sliding doors opening onto the patio, this welcoming area is easily served by the L-shaped kitchen which shares a snack bar with the dining room. The three bedrooms are separated from the living areas by the careful placement of the bathrooms and the laundry. The master bedroom features two closets, including a walk-in, plus a private bath. This plan comes with a basement or crawlspace foundation, please specify when ordering

Main living area — 1,440 sq. ft.
Garage — 2-car

Total living area — 1,440 sq. ft.

No. 90125

Plant Shelf Divides Living Space with Greenery

No. 90394

Twin gables, a beautiful half-round window, and Colonial-style corner boards give this one-story classic an inviting, traditional exterior that says "Welcome". Inside, the ingenious, open plan of active areas makes every room seem even larger. Look at the vaulted living room, where floor-to-ceiling windows provide a pleasing unity with the yard. In the spectacular dining room, which adjoins the kitchen for convenient mealtimes, sliding glass doors open to a rear deck. Three bedrooms at the rear of the house include the angular master suite, which features a private bath and double-sized closet.

Main living area — 1,252 sq. ft.
Garage — 2-car

No. 90394

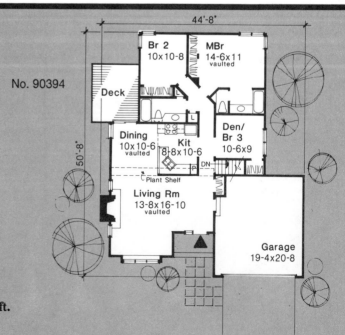

Total living area — 1,252 sq. ft.

Built-Ins Add Extra Storage Space

No. 90207

This versatile, one-level plan keeps active and quiet areas separate for maximum privacy. A massive fireplace with raised hearth divides the central entry from the huge gathering room. Notice how common areas flow together.. Three sliding doors off the gathering and dining rooms and the glass walls of the bayed breakfast nook combine with this open arrangement to create a spacious feeling throughout the area. Need warm weather living space? Retreat to the surrounding rear terrace for stargazing or a candlelit dinner. A hallway tucked off the entry leads to three bedrooms and two full baths. You'll appreciate the generous closet space and the private terrace access in the master suite.

Main living area — 1,366 sq. ft.

Garage — 2-car

Total living area — 1,366 sq. ft.

No. 90207

Fireplace Dominates Rustic Design

No. 90409

The ample porch, of this charming home deserves a rocking chair, and there's room for two or three if you'd like. The front entry opens to an expansive Great room with a soaring cathedral ceiling. Flanked by the master suite and two bedrooms with a full bath, the Great room is separated from formal dining by a massive fireplace. The convenient galley kitchen adjoins a sunny breakfast nook, perfect for informal family dining. This plan comes with either a basement, crawlspace or slab foundation, please specify which you would like when ordering.

Main living area — 1,670 sq. ft.
Garage — 2-car

Total living area — 1,670 sq. ft.

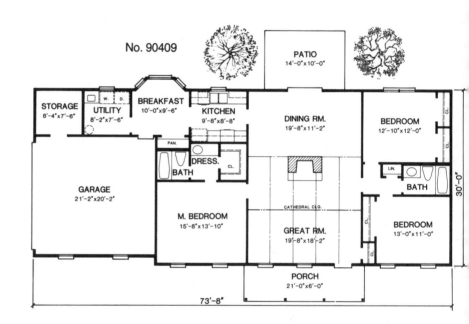

No. 90409

PATIO 14'-0" x 10'-0"

STORAGE 8'-4" x 7'-6"

W. D. UTILITY 8'-2" x 7'-6"

BREAKFAST 10'-0" x 9'-6"

KITCHEN 9'-8" x 8'-8"

PAN.

DINING RM. 19'-8" x 11'-2"

BEDROOM 12'-10" x 12'-0"

DRESS.

BATH

CL.

LIN.

BATH

GARAGE 21'-2" x 20'-2"

M. BEDROOM 15'-8" x 13'-10"

CATHEDRAL CLG.

GREAT RM. 19'-8" x 18'-2"

BEDROOM 13'-0" x 11'-0"

PORCH 21'-0" x 6'-0"

73'-8"

30'-0"

Detailed Ranch Design

No. 90360

Stylish houses, to suit the higher design expectations of the sophisticated first-time and move-up buyers, need to present a lot of visible values. Starting with the very modern exterior look of this home with its arcaded living room sash, through its interior vaulted spaces and interesting master bedroom suite, this house says "buy me". Foundation offsets are kept to the front where they count for character; simple main roof frames over main house body and master bedroom are cantilevered. Note, too, the easy option of eliminating the third bedroom closet and opening this room to the kitchen as a family room plus two bedroom home.

Main living area — 1,283 sq. ft.

Total living area — 1,283 sq. ft.

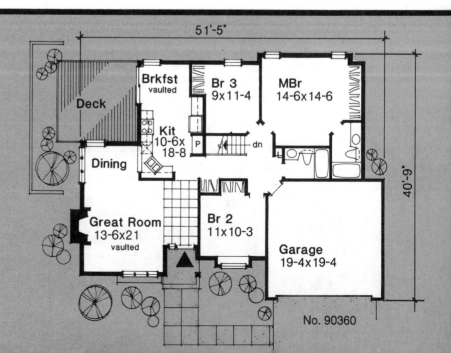

51'-5"

Deck

Brkfst vaulted

Br 3 9x11-4

MBr 14-6x14-6

Kit 10-6x 18-8

Dining

P

dn

40'-9"

Great Room 13-6x21 vaulted

Br 2 11x10-3

Garage 19-4x19-4

No. 90360

Compact Home is Surprisingly Spacious

No. 90905

Searching for a design where the living room takes advantage of both front and rear views? Look no further. And, this cozy ranch has loads of other features. An attractive porch welcomes guests and provides shade for the big living room window on hot summer days. A large covered sundeck adjacent to the living room, dining room and kitchen will make entertaining a delight. The roomy bedrooms, including the master suite with full bath and a walk-in closet, are protected from street noise by the two-car garage.

Main floor — 1,314 sq. ft.
Unfinished basement — 1,488 sq. ft.
Garage — 484 sq. ft.
Width — 50'-0"
Depth — 54'-0"

Total living area — 1,314 sq. ft.

No. 90905

Lots of Living Space in Compact Design

No. 90368

Smaller houses can use detailed treatment and a sense of scale to take on the look and character of larger homes. You'll love the looks and perceived value from this minimum expenditure design. The open living spaces, rear yard views, and luxurious master bedroom suite, will have the essential lifestyle characteristics of a larger home.

Main living area — 1,081 sq. ft.

Total living area — 1,081 sq. ft.

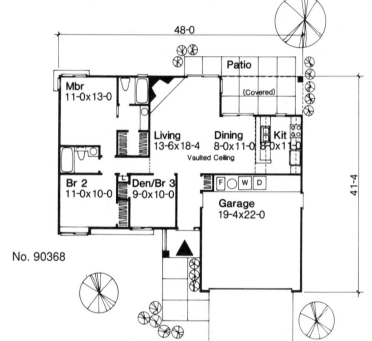

No. 90368

Small With Room To Grow

No. 20205

This contemporary is perfect for the young family starting out. It has three bedrooms and the master suite has a vaulted ceiling and its own master bath. The secondary bedrooms have ample closet space and share the hallway bath. The fireplace in the living room adds the warmth and atmosphere needed on cold winter evenings. The lower level offers an optional room to be used as a rec room or whatever your growing family needs. Although it may be smaller, this home does not scrimp on style.

Lower level — 286 sq. ft.
Main level — 1,321 sq. ft.
Garage — 655 sq. ft.

Total living area — 1,607 sq. ft.

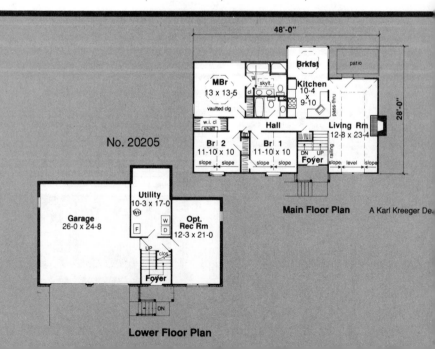

No. 20205

Main Floor Plan   A Karl Kreeger De...

Lower Floor Plan

Students Love the Alcove

No. 91351

Starting at the sheltered entry, this home with its
many appealing features, lends itself well to those
desiring comfortable family living. The well
planned layout is ideal for today's growing
family. This single level traditional styled home
has a total of 1,477 sq. ft. and there are two
distinctive elevations from which to choose. The
entry opens to the living room that is enhanced
by a stone hearth fireplace. It flows into the
dining room, with built-in shelves, or to the
family room, open to the efficiently designed
kitchen. The master bedroom suite is complete
with walk-in closet, double sink vanity, and a
private shower. Bedrooms two and three are
served by a full bath located in the hall. Note the
study alcove in bedroom number three. The
efficient compact laundry room leads to the
double car garage that also has a side entry door.
A porch at the rear of the house is perfect for
entertaining, and can be accessed from either the
master bedroom suite or the family room.

Main living area — 1,477 sq. ft.
Garage — 2-car

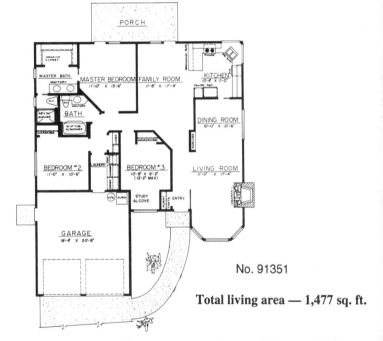

No. 91351

Total living area — 1,477 sq. ft.

Great Room Has Vaulted Ceiling

No. 90361

The triple appeal of stylish impact, a great kitchen with charming breakfast area, and a luxurious master bedroom suite give this house high perceived value in today's very competitive mid-priced marketplace. Note how these features are emphasized with balconied stairs overlooking living and dining rooms, greenhouse plus bay windowed kitchen, and master bath with platform tub, stall shower, and oversized walk-in closet. Combined with the highly detailed, custom-look exterior, this total design package gives you a lot for your money.

First floor — 1,105 sq. ft.
Second floor — 460 sq. ft.

Total living area — 1,565 sq. ft.

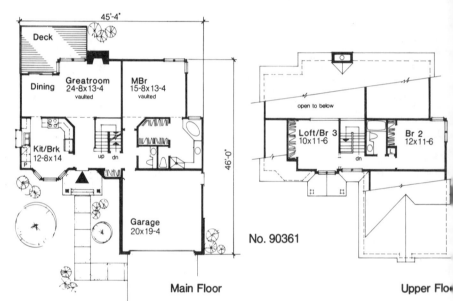

No. 90361

Main Floor   Upper Floor

Nostalgic Charm

No. 99317

This home combines contemporary features such as dramatic vaulted ceilings, loft, well-equipped kitchen and energy efficiency. Outside, the nostalgic character is created by the covered front porch, curved arch and decorative support posts, lattice trim, divided sash and stone chimney accent. Inside, the vaulted foyer opens to the sunken living room with fireplace, vaulted ceiling with loft overlook, corner windows with transom glass above, and a focal point library alcove with quaint window seat.

Main floor — 744 sq. ft.
Upper floor — 833 sq. ft.
Garage — 2-car

Total living area — 1,577 sq. ft.

No. 99317

Main Floor   Upper Floor

Another Nice Ranch Design

No. 90354

Small and move-up houses are looking much larger these days thanks to clever proportions and roof masses, as exemplified in this two-bedroom ranch. The inside space seems larger, from the high-impact entrance with through-views to the vaulted Great room, fireplace, and rear deck. The den (optional third bedroom) features double doors. The kitchen and breakfast area has a vaulted ceiling. The plan easily adapts to crawl or slab construction with utilities replacing stairs, laundry facing the kitchen and air handler and water heater facing the garage.

Main living area — 1,360 sq. ft.
Garage — 2-car

Total living area — 1,360 sq. ft.

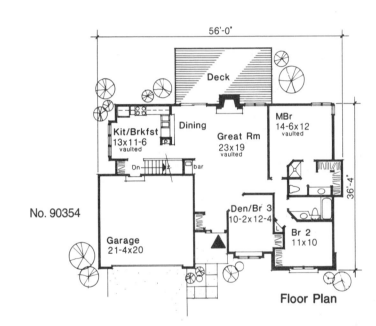

No. 90354

56'-0"

Deck

Kit/Brkfst
13x11-6
vaulted

Dining

Great Rm
23x19
vaulted

MBr
14-6x12
vaulted

Dn

bar

36'-4"

Garage
21-4x20

Den/Br 3
10-2x12-4

Br 2
11x10

Floor Plan

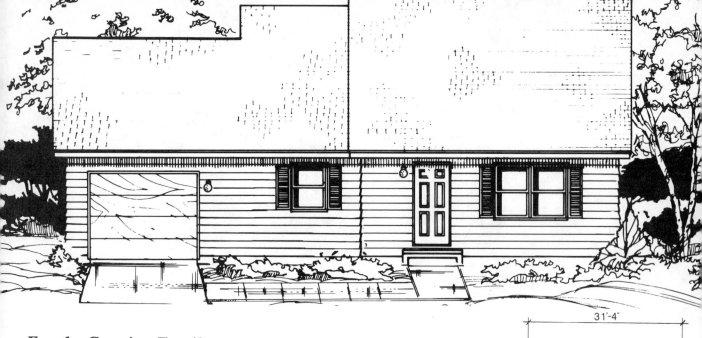

For the Growing Family

No. 92032

Here's an 1,104 sq. ft. one-and-a-half story plan
that has plenty of room to grow into. The single
car attached garage has plenty of storage space.
The main floor, with it's large formal living
room, also features a large U-shaped kitchen,
formal dining room, main floor laundry facilities,
bedroom and 3/4 bath. Upstairs features two
bedrooms and a bath.

Lower level — 715 sq. ft.
Upper level — 389 sq. ft.
Garage — 1-car

4 or More Occupants
Total living area — 1,104 sq. ft.

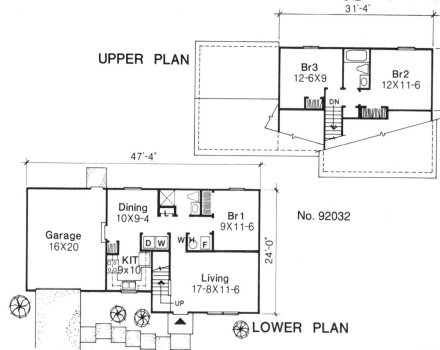

Lots of Living Space in a Small Package

No. 92040

This 846 sq. ft. 2-bedroom ranch plan offers a lot
of living space in a small package. The large
living room is open to the U-shaped kitchen and
dining area, with easy access to the single-car
attached garage for ease of carrying groceries.
The plan also features a large laundry/utility
room.

Main living area — 846 sq. ft.
Garage — 1-car

Total living area — 846 sq. ft.
1 or More Occupants

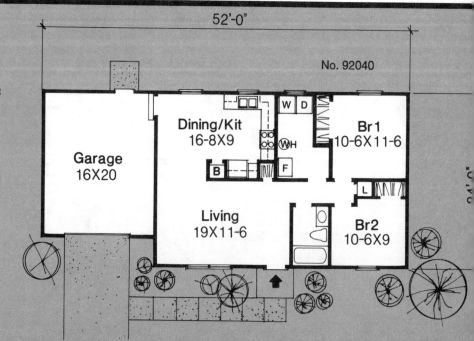

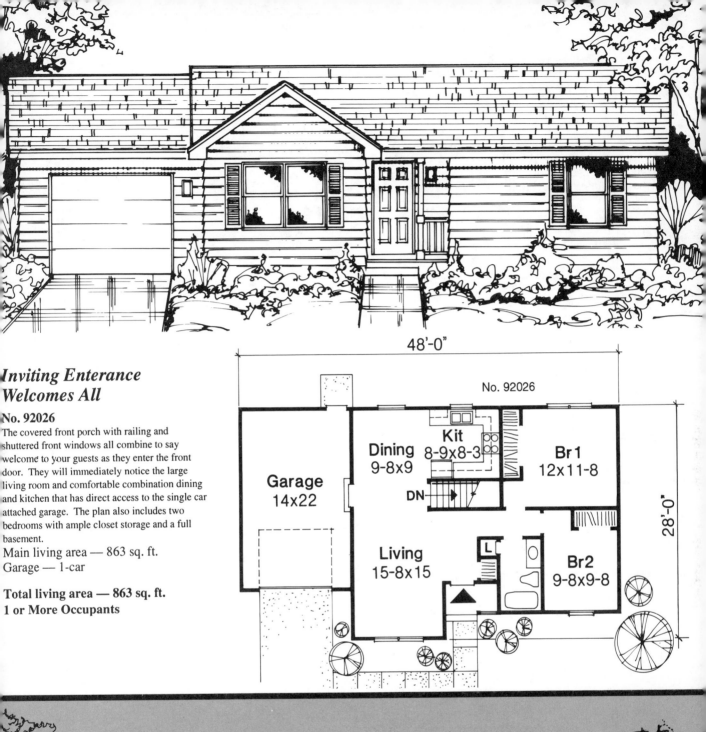

Inviting Enterance Welcomes All

No. 92026

The covered front porch with railing and shuttered front windows all combine to say welcome to your guests as they enter the front door. They will immediately notice the large living room and comfortable combination dining and kitchen that has direct access to the single car attached garage. The plan also includes two bedrooms with ample closet storage and a full basement.

Main living area — 863 sq. ft.
Garage — 1-car

Total living area — 863 sq. ft.
1 or More Occupants

48'-0"

No. 92026

Garage 14x22

Dining 9-8x9

Kit 8-9x8-3

Br 1 12x11-8

DN

Living 15-8x15

L

Br2 9-8x9-8

28'-0"

Bedrooms Located on Second Level

No. 90369

Today's houses of modest size are being designed with the impact of formerly much larger designs. This two-story is just such a concept with a vaulted ceiling in its living room up to the hall balcony above, the triple room accommodation of living room, dining room, and family room, the luxurious master bath and closet, and the long low sweep of roof lines. Note, too, the design importance centered around the front porch and entry, and the carefully proportioned sash on all four elevations to make this house look good from every angle. Masonry accents help further tie the house to its site.

First floor — 888 sq. ft.
Second floor — 776 sq. ft.
Garage — 2-car

Total living area — 1,664 sq. ft.

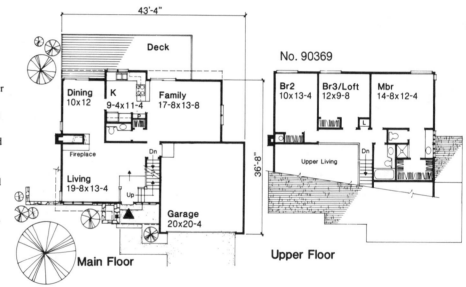

Main Floor

Upper Floor

No. 90369

43'-4"

Deck

Dining 10x12

K 9-4x11-4

Family 17-8x13-8

Fireplace

Living 19-8x13-4

Dn

Up

Garage 20x20-4

36'-8"

Br2 10x13-4

Br3/Loft 12x9-8

Mbr 14-8x12-4

Upper Living

Dn

Family Plan

No. 91504

With four bedrooms and a wealth of open space, this home is ideal for your growing family. The two-story foyer sets the stage for the spacious feeling you'll find throughout the house. Formal areas flow together in a sunny arrangement accentuated by a bay window in the living room. You'll find a similar treatment in the family areas at the rear of the house, where the island kitchen, breakfast nook, and family room all benefit from a vaulted ceiling crowned by a fireplace and lots of windows overlooking the backyard. Four bedrooms and two baths lie up the L-shaped staircase that ascends from the foyer. Notice the elegant skylit bath and generous closet space in the master suite.

First floor — 1,105 sq. ft.
Second floor — 950 sq. ft.
Garage — 2-car

Total living area — 2,055 sq. ft.

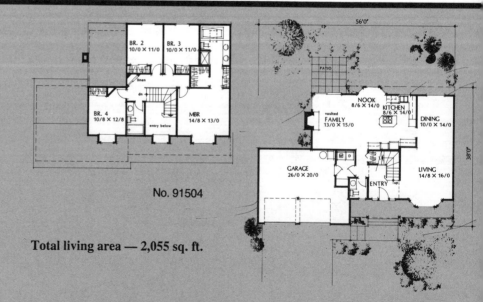

No. 91504

56'0"

BR. 2 10/0 × 11/0

BR. 3 10/0 × 11/0

linen

BR. 4 10/8 × 12/8

dn

entry below

MBR 14/8 × 13/0

PATIO

NOOK 8/6 × 14/0

KITCHEN 8/6 × 14/0

vaulted FAMILY 13/0 × 15/0

DINING 10/0 × 14/0

GARAGE 26/0 × 20/0

W D

ENTRY

LIVING 14/8 × 16/0

38'0"

Design Offers Customized Features

No. 90362

Family homes today need all the luxury features of a custom home to capture the buyer's attention. This home is full of those features; walk-in, pass-thru wetbar; vaulted Great room with featured fireplace; deluxe master bedroom-bath suite; convenient laundry with counter space; dormered loft; etc. Plus, the exterior looks importantly large, with variegated roof line interest, transom glass Great room bay window, and protective front entry porch.

First floor — 1,290 sq. ft.
Second floor — 664 sq. ft.
Garage — 2-car

Total living area — 1,954 sq. ft.

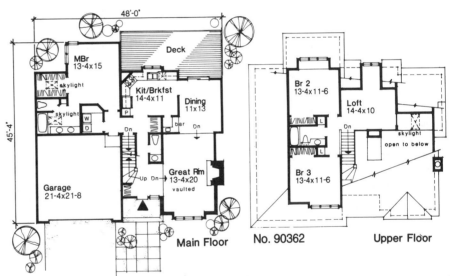

Main Floor

No. 90362   Upper Floor

Single-Level Living

No. 99329

For the move-up or empty-nester buyer who is looking for lots of features, but wants them all on one floor, consider this 1,642 square foot home. The interior offers many surprises like a vaulted ceiling in the living room and a built-in plant shelf. A fireplace forms the focus of this room. The angled kitchen has a sunny breakfast room. The formal dining room has stately divider details. Two bedrooms and two full baths in the sleeping wing of the home include the master suite.

Main living area — 1,642 sq. ft.
Garage — 2-car

Total living area — 1,642 sq. ft.

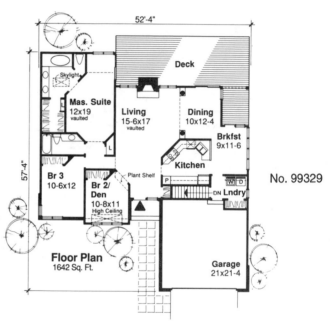

No. 99329

Floor Plan
1642 Sq. Ft.

Adaptable For the Disabled

No. 91652

The charming and cozy exterior of this two-plus bedroom, two bath home does not prepare you for the drama within. Elegant arched doorways lead you to the living and family rooms. Entertain in the dining room, warm up to a cozy fireplace or study in the den; comfort abounds in every room of this warm home. Designed as a lifetime home, it is handicap accessible and has convenient, luxurious features such as an expansive kitchen with walk-in pantry and breakfast nook, and a large walk-in closet in the master bedroom.

Main living area — 1,541 sq. ft.
Garage — 2-car

Total living area — 1,541 sq. ft.

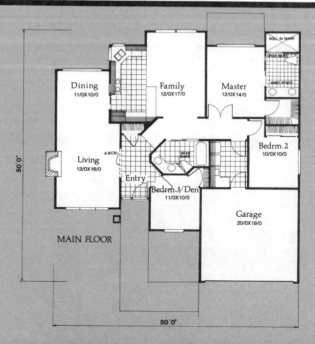

No. 91652

Contemporary with a Country Flair

No. 20203

This three bedroom contemporary has a welcoming country porch. Although this home is classified as small, it has alot of potential for a growing family. As you enter the foyer you can look into the living room at a glowing fire or turn right and find out what's cooking for dinner in the efficient kitchen. The kitchen also features your washer and dryer, a pantry and bowed breakfast nook. The master suite has a decor ceiling, walk-in closet and its own master bath. The dining room also has a decor ceiling to add interest. Upstairs the secondary bedrooms share a full bath.

First floor — 1,229 sq. ft.
Second floor — 515 sq. ft.
Garage — 452 sq. ft.

Total living area — 1,744 sq. ft.

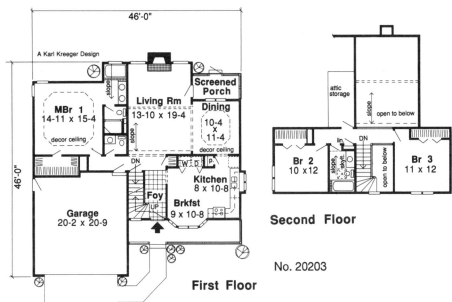

46'-0"

A Karl Kreeger Design

Screened Porch

MBr 1
14-11 x 15-4
decor ceiling

Living Rm
13-10 x 19-4

Dining
10-4 x 11-4
decor ceiling

46'-0"

Garage
20-2 x 20-9

DN

Foy
UP

W D P

Kitchen
8 x 10-8

Brkfst
9 x 10-8

First Floor

attic storage

open to below

slope

Br 2
10 x 12

lin.

DN

open to below

Br 3
11 x 12

Second Floor

No. 20203

Have Your Morning Coffee on the Sundeck

No. 90911

If you've been searching for a contemporary home at a price you can afford, you must consider this exciting model. Interesting exterior angles are enhanced by the clean lines of cedar plank siding. The front entrance is sheltered by a roof extension and leads into a sunny foyer. Walk up to the main level, brightened by lots of oversized windows. The big double garage includes a large storage and workshop area with convenient access to the rear yard. If you like modern styling, this three-bedroom beauty will reflect your good taste.

Main floor — 1,205 sq. ft.
Basement — 550 sq. ft.
Garage — 728 sq. ft.
Width — 46'-0"
Depth — 32'-0"

Total living area — 1,205 sq. ft.

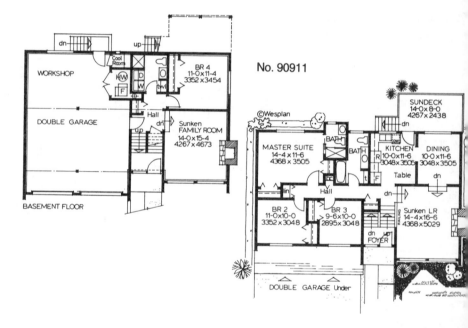

No. 90911

Designed for the TV Buff

No. 90621

No matter where you decide to build, you'll be sure to get perfect TV reception in the living room of this passive solar home. A satellite dish shares south-facing roof space with skylights and hot water solar collectors. The entertainment center is visible from all the living areas, grouped together in an open space. The entrance foyer leads to the main rooms and the master bedroom off the bathroom hall. The upstairs hall, two bedrooms, and bath are brightened by clerestory windows. With energy-saving construction features, this home will give you years of enjoyment with minimal energy costs.

First floor (excluding deck) — 967 sq. ft.
Second floor — 389 sq. ft.

Total living area — 1,356 sq. ft.

SECOND FLOOR PLAN

FIRST FLOOR PLAN

No. 90621

A Home for All Season

No. 90629

The natural cedar and stone exterior of this contemporary gem is virtually maintenance free, and its dramatic lines echo the excitement inside. There are so many luxurious touches in this plan: the two-story living room overlooked by an upper-level balcony, a massive stone wall that pierces the roof and holds two fireplaces, a kitchen oven and an outdoor barbecue. Outdoor dining is a pleasure with the barbecue so handy to the kitchen. All the rooms boast outdoor decks, and each bedroom has its own. The front entrance, garage, a dressing room with bath, and laundry room occupy the lower level.

Main level — 1,001 sq. ft.
Upper level — 712 sq. ft.
Lower level — 463 sq. ft.
Garage — 2-car

Total living area — 2,176 sq. ft.

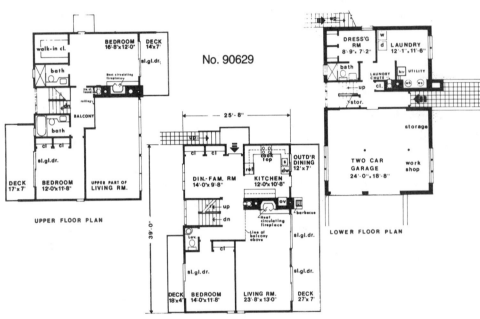

No. 90629

UPPER FLOOR PLAN

walk-in cl.	BEDROOM 16'-8"x12'-0"	DECK 14'x7'
bath	Heat circulating fireplace	sl.gl.dr.
bath	BALCONY	
DECK 17'x7'	BEDROOM 12'-0"x11'-8"	UPPER PART OF LIVING RM.

MAIN FLOOR PLAN

25'-8"
39'-0"

DIN.-FAM. RM 14'-0"x9'-8"
KITCHEN 12'-0"x10'-8"
OUTD'R DINING 12'x7'
barbecue
Heat circulating fireplace
Line of balcony above
LIVING RM. 23'-8"x13'-0"
BEDROOM 14'-0"x11'-8"
DECK 18'x4'
DECK 27'x7'

LOWER FLOOR PLAN

DRESS'G RM 8'-9", 7'-2"
LAUNDRY 12'-1", 11'-6"
bath
LAUNDRY CHUTE
UTILITY
storage
TWO CAR GARAGE 24'-0", 18'-8"
work shop

Distinctive Split-Level

No. 90010

From its dramatically handsome entrance to the master bedroom's spacious walk-in closet, this home is distinctive in every detail. Exterior appearance is luxerious, with stone, brick and wood shingles excellently combined. The large foyer serves as a traffic hub. A sunken garden outside the large family room is reached through sliding glass doors. The efficient kitchen includes a breakfast balcony overlooking the family room. The bedroom area is served by two complete baths. Another half bath serves the family room area.

Main living area — 1,727 sq. ft.

Total living area — 1,727 sq. ft.

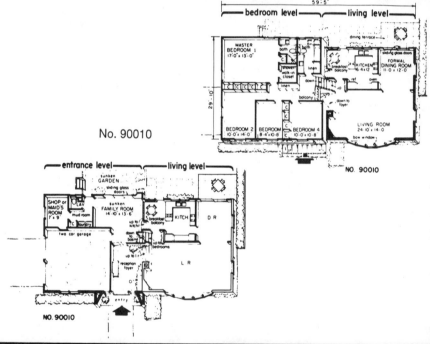

No. 90010

Rustic Design Blends with Hillside

No. 10012

Naturally perfect for a woodland setting, this redwood decked home will adapt equally well to a lake or ocean setting. A car or boat garage is furnished on the lower level. Fireplaces equip both the living room and the 36-foot long family room which opens onto a shaded patio. A laundry room adjoins the open kitchen which shares the large redwood deck encircling the living and dining area. Two bedrooms and two full baths on the first floor supplement another bedroom and half bath on the lower level.

Main living area — 1,198 sq. ft.
Basement — 1,198 sq. ft.

Total living area — 1,198 sq. ft.

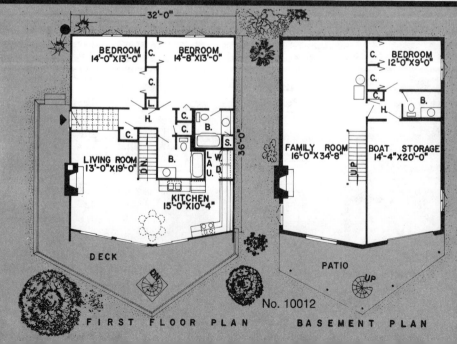

No. 10012

FIRST FLOOR PLAN   BASEMENT PLAN

Cozy Cape Cod

No. 90115

The living and dining rooms in this home are completely separated from the family room, enabling adults and children to enjoy undisturbed everyday living. Notice the location of the first floor bath in relation to the dining room —a plan feature that permits this room to be used as a first floor bedroom, if desired. Back service entrance, mud room and laundry convenient to the kitchen are favorable points of the plan, too. On the second floor, the huge master bedroom has its own dressing area and entrance to the vanity bath. This plan is available with a basement or crawlspace/slab foundation. Please specify when ordering.

First floor — 1,068 sq. ft.
Second floor — 804 sq. ft.
Garage — 1 or 2-car

Total living area — 1,872 sq. ft.

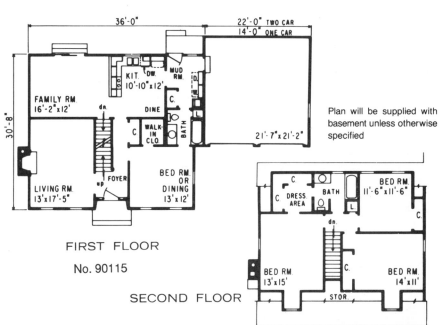

Plan will be supplied with basement unless otherwise specified

FIRST FLOOR

No. 90115

SECOND FLOOR

Extra Roof Lines Give Traditional Appeal

No. 20202

Sloped ceilings in the living room and dining room give added dimension to this charming Traditional. In the breakfast nook, note the bi-fold doors that keep the washer and dryer hidden. The master bedroom, complete with decorative ceiling, leads into an elegant his-and-hers master bath with tub, shower and oversized walk-in closet. Three bedrooms on the second level share a full bath and each have ample closet space. An ornamental plant shelf amplifies the beauty of the open space overlooking the living room and dining room.

First floor — 1,205 sq. ft.
Second floor — 680 sq. ft.
Garage — 480 sq. ft.

Total living area — 1,885 sq. ft.

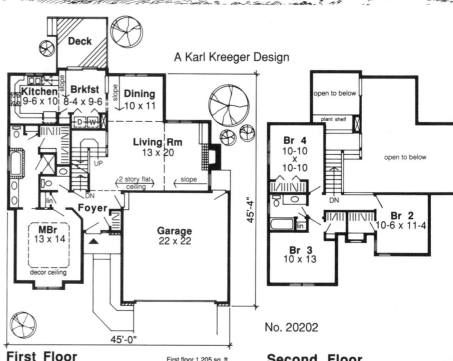

A Karl Kreeger Design

Deck

Kitchen 9-6 x 10
Brkfst 8-4 x 9-6
Dining 10 x 11
Living Rm 13 x 20
2 story flat ceiling
slope
D W
UP
DN
Foyer
MBr 13 x 14
decor ceiling
Garage 22 x 22

45'-0"

First Floor   First floor 1,205 sq. ft.

open to below
plant shelf
Br 4 10-10 x 10-10
open to below
DN
Br 2 10-6 x 11-4
Br 3 10 x 13
lin
45'-4"

No. 20202

Second Floor

Abundance of Closet Space

No. 20204

Each of the three bedrooms in this roomy ranch has its own walk-in closet for added convenience. Two bedrooms share a full bath, while the master bedroom has a private bath featuring tub and shower. Also included in the layout of the master bedroom is a unique closet used to house the washer and dryer, affording ease of first-floor laundering. Sloped ceilings in the fireplaced living room give added height and sliders lead out to a large deck. The kitchen is surrounded by plenty of cupboard space and also includes a convenient pantry for extra storage.

Main living area — 1,532 sq. ft.
Garage — 484 sq. ft.

Total living area — 1,532 sq. ft.

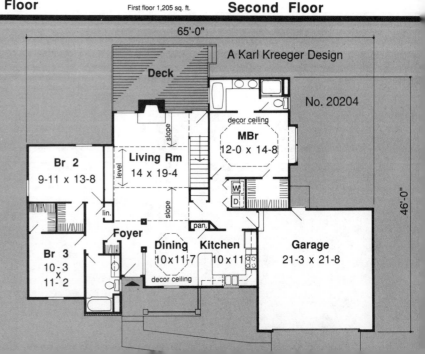

65'-0"

A Karl Kreeger Design

Deck

No. 20204

decor ceiling
MBr 12-0 x 14-8
Br 2 9-11 x 13-8
Living Rm 14 x 19-4
slope
level
slope
W D
lin
pan.
Foyer
Br 3 10-3 x 11-2
Dining 10 x 11-7
Kitchen 10 x 11
Garage 21-3 x 21-8
decor ceiling

46'-0"

From Times Gone By

No. 24301

Reminiscent of a simplier time, yet up-to-date on the conveniences we have come to depend on. The front porch is a warm welcome at the end of the day. Come inside to the large living room, great for entertaining. Or relax in your family room which opens to your deck. Upstairs the master bedroom has its own bath and ample closet space. The secondary bedrooms, of which there are three, share the hall bath and each have lots of closet space. Family living at its best!

Main level — 985 sq. ft.
Upper level — 970 sq. ft.
Basement — 985 sq. ft.
Garage — 2-car

Total living area — 1,955 sq. ft.

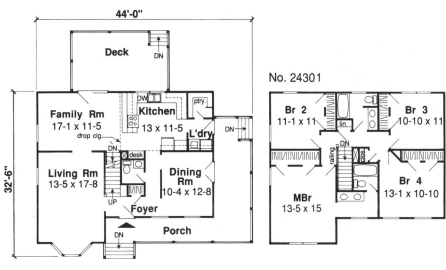

First Floor   Second Floor

Everything you need to make your dream come true!

You pay only a fraction of the original cost for home designs by respected professionals.

You've picked your dream home!

You can already see it standing on your lot... you can see yourselves in your new home... enjoying family, entertaining guests, celebrating holidays. All that remains ahead are the details. That's where we can help.

Whether you plan to build-it-yourself, be your own contractor, or hand your plans over to an outside contractor, your Garlinghouse blueprints provide the perfect beginning for putting yourself in your dream home right away.

We even make it simple for you to make professional design modifications. We can also provide a materials list for greater economy.

My grandfather, L.F. Garlinghouse, started a tradition of quality when he founded this company in 1907. For over 85 years, homeowners and builders have relied on us for accurate, complete, professional blueprints. Our plans help you get results fast... and save money, too! These pages will give you all the information you need to order. So get started now... I know you'll love your new Garlinghouse home!

Sincerely,

Here's What You Get!

1 Exterior Elevations
Exact scale views of the front, rear, and both sides of your home, showing exterior materials, details, and all necessary measurements.

2 Detailed Floor Plans
Showing the placement of all interior walls, the dimensions of rooms, doors, windows, stairways, and other details.

3 Foundation Plan
With footings and all load-bearing points as applicable to your home, including all necessary notations and dimensions. The foundation style supplied varies from home to home. Local conditions and practices will determine whether a basement, crawl-space, or a slab is best for you. Your professional contractor can easily make the necessary adaption.

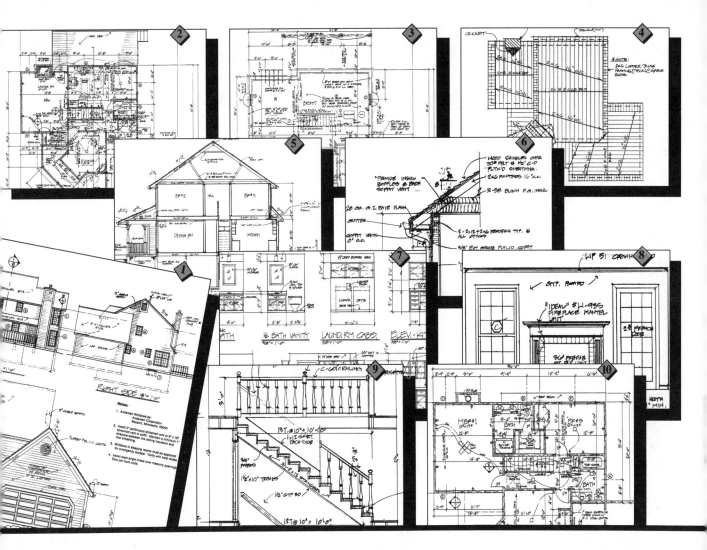

◆4 *Roof Plan*

All information necessary to construct the roof for your home is included. Many blueprints contain framing plans showing all of the roof elements, so you'll know how these details look and fit together.

◆5 *Typical Cross-Section*

A detailed, full cross-sectional view through the entire house, as if the house was cut from top to bottom. This elevation allows a contractor to better understand the interconnections of the construction components.

◆6 *Typical Wall Sections*

Detailed views of your exterior wall, as though sliced from top to bottom. These drawings clarify exterior wall construction, insulation, flooring, and roofing details. Depending on your specific geography and climate, your home will be built with either 2x4 or 2x6 exterior walls. Most professional contractors can easily adapt plans for either requirement.

◆7 *Kitchen & Bath Cabinet Details*

These plans or, in some cases, elevations show the specific details and placement of the cabinets in your kitchen and bathrooms, as applicable. Customizing these areas is simpler beginning with these details.

◆8 *Fireplace Details*

When your home includes one or more fireplaces, these detailed drawings will help your mason with their construction and appearance. It is easy to review details with professionals when you have the plans for reference.

◆9 *Stair Details*

If stairs are part of the design you selected, specific plans are included for their construction and details.

◆10 *Schematic Electrical Layouts*

The suggested locations for all of your switches, outlets, and fixtures

are indicated on these drawings. They are practical as they are, but they are also a solid taking-off point for any personal adaptions.

Also available, is a money-saving Materials List.

Plus...

FREE

Specifications and Contract Form

FREE

14-page Energy Conservation Guide.

TURN THE PAGE FOR THE EASY STEPS TO COMPLETE YOUR DREAM HOME ORDER!

Garlinghouse options and extras make the dream truly yours.

Reversed Plans Can Make Your Dream Home Just Right!

"That's our dream home... if only the garage were on the other side!"

You could have exactly the home you want by flipping it end-for-end. Check it out by holding your dream home page of this book up to a mirror. Then simply order your plans "reversed". We'll send you one full set of mirror-image plans (with the writing backwards) as a master guide for you and your builder.

The remaining sets of your order will come as shown in this book so the dimensions and specifications are easily read on the job site... but they will be specially stamped "REVERSED" so there is no construction confusion.

We can only send reversed plans with multiple-set orders. But, there is no extra charge for this service.

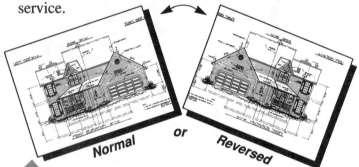

Normal or Reversed

Modifying Your Garlinghouse Home Plan

Easy modifications to your dream home... minor non-structural changes, simple materials substitutions... can be made between you and your builder.

However, if you are considering making major changes to your design, we strongly recommend that you use an architect or a professional designer. And, since you have already started with our complete detailed blueprints, the cost of those expensive professional services will be significantly less.

Our Reproducible Vellums Make Modifications Easier

They provide a design professional with the right way to make changes directly to your Garlinghouse home plans and then print as many copies of the modified plans as you need. The price is $395 plus shipping. Call 1-800-235-5700 to find out more.

Remember To Order Your Materials List

It'll help you save money. Available at a modest additional charge, the Materials List gives the quantity, dimensions, and specifications for the major materials needed to build your home. You will get faster, more accurate bids from your contractors and building suppliers — and avoid paying for unused materials and waste. Materials Lists are available for all home plans except as otherwise indicated, but can only be ordered with a set of home plans. Due to differences in local building codes, regional requirements, and homeowner/builder preferences... electrical, plumbing & heating/air conditioning equipment requirements aren't provided.

How Many Sets Of Plans Will You Need?

The Standard 8-Set Construction Package

Our experience shows that you'll speed every step of construction and avoid costly building errors by ordering enough sets to go around. Each tradesperson wants a set — the general contractor and all subcontractors; foundation, electrical, plumbing, heating/air conditioning, drywall, finish carpenters, and cabinet shop. Don't forget your lending institution, building deparment and, of course, a set for yourself.

The Minimum 5-Set Construction Package

If you're comfortable with arduous follow-up, this package can save you a few dollars. You might have enough copies to go around if work goes exactly as scheduled and no plans are lost or damaged. But for only $30 more, the 8-set package eliminates these worries.

The Single-Set Decision-Maker Package

We offer this set so you can study the blueprints to plan your dream home in detail. But remember... one set is never enough to build your home... and they're copyrighted.

Questions?

Call our customer service number at 1-203-632-0500.
An important note:

All plans are drawn to conform to one or more of the industry's major national building standards. However, due to the variety of local building regulations, your plan may need to be modified to comply with local requirements — snow loads, energy loads, seismic zones, etc. Do check them fully and consult your local building officials.

A few states require that all building plans used be drawn by an architect registered in that state. While having your plans reviewed and stamped by such an architect may be prudent, laws requiring non-conforming plans like ours to be completely redrawn forces you to unnecessarily pay very large fees. If your state has such a law, we strongly recommend you contact your state representative to protest.

Important Shipping Information

Your order is processed immediately. Allow 10 working days from our receipt of your order for normal UPS delivery. Save time with your credit card and our "800" number. UPS *must* have a street address or Rural Route Box number — never a post office box. Use a work address if no one is home during the day.

Orders being shipped to Alaska, Hawaii, APO, FPO or Post Office Boxes must go via First Class Mail. Please include the proper postage.

Canadian Orders and Shipping:

To our friends in Canada, we have a plan design affiliate in Kitchener, Ontario. This relationship will help you avoid the delays and charges associated with shipments from the United States. Morever, our affiliate is familiar with the building requirements in your community and country.

We prefer payments in U.S. Currency. If you, however, are sending Canadian funds, please add 25% to the prices of the plans and shipping fees.

Domestic Shipping (stated in U.S. dollars)	
UPS Ground Service	$ 7.00
First Class Mail	$ 8.50
Express Delivery Service Call For Details 1-800-235-5700	

International Shipping (stated in U.S. dollars)	One Set	Mult. Sets
Canada	$7.25	$12.50
All Other Nations	$18.50	$50.00

Canadian Orders are now Duty Free

Please submit all Canadian plan orders to:

The Garlinghouse Company, Inc.
20 Cedar Street North
Kitchener, Ontario N2H, 2W8
Canadian orders only: 1-800-561-4169
Fax #: 1-519-743-1282
Customer Service #: 1-519-743-4169

Mexico and Other Countries:

If you are ordering from outside the United States, please note that your check, money order, or international money transfer **must be payable in U.S. currency.** For speed, we ship international orders Air Parcel Post. Please refer to the chart for the correct shipping cost.

Blueprint Price Schedule (stated in U.S. dollars)	
Standard Constuction Package (8 sets)	$255.00
Minimum Construction Package (5 sets)	225.00
Single-Set Package (no reverses)	180.00
Each Additional Set (ordered w/one above)	20.00
Materials List (with plan order only)	25.00

ORDER TOLL FREE — 1-800-235-5700

Monday-Friday 8:00am to 5:00pm Eastern Time
or FAX your Credit Card order to (203)632-0712
All other nations
call 1-203-632-0500. Please have the
following at your fingertips before you call:

1. *Your credit card number*
2. *The plan number*
3. *The order code number*

Blueprint Order Form   Order Code #H3SM5

Plan No. _____

❏ As Shown ❏ Reversed *(mult. set pkgs. only)*

	Each	Amount
8 set pkg.	$255.00	$
5 set pkg.	$225.00	$
1 set pkg.*(no reverses)*	$180.00	$
___(Qty.) Add. sets @	$ 20.00	$
Material List	$ 25.00	$
Shipping — see chart		$
Subtotal		$
Sales Tax (CT residents add 6% sales tax, KS residents add 5.9% sales tax)		$
Total Amount Enclosed		$

Thank you for your order!

Send your check, money order or credit card information to:

Garlinghouse Company
34 Industrial Park Place, P.O. Box 1717
Middletown, CT 06457

Bill To: *(address must be as it appears on credit card statement)*

Name _____
          (Please Print)

Address _____

City/State _____ Zip _____

Daytime Phone ( ) _____

Ship To *(if different from Bill to):*

Name _____

Address _____
          (UPS will not ship to P.O. Boxes)

City/State _____ Zip _____

Credit Card Information

Charge To: ❏ Mastercard ❏ Visa ❏ Discover

Card #|_|_|_|_|_|_|_|_|_|_|_|_|_|_|_|_|_|_|

Signature _____ Exp. ___/___

BUILD-IT-YOURSELF BOOKS

These books have been written to help the do-it-yourselfer turn a dream home into reality. Most are hard to find information sources designed to give you the expertise necessary to build all or part of your new dream home, yourself. No matter how involved you intend to be in the construction process, having a clear understanding of how your home goes together is the only way to insure that the finished house is properly built.

BOOK NO. 2510
MODERN CARPENTRY

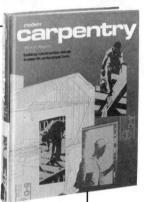

With ample color photographs and illustrations, this book thoroughly explains how to frame, insulate, build foundations, fireplaces and chimneys, and even how to add passive solar features to your home. If you want to learn how a home is built, then this book is required reading. 492 pp.; over 1400 illus.; Goodheart - Willcox (hardcover)

$31.00

BOOK NO. 2508
MODERN PLUMBING

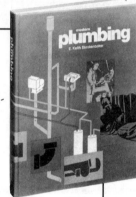

All aspects of plumbing installation, as well as service and repairs, are presented here in generously illustrated, easy to follow text. Heating and air conditioning installation are another major aspect of this hard to find book. 300 pp.; over 700 illus.; Goodheart - Willcox (hardcover)

$24.60

BOOK NO. 2546
BLUEPRINT READING FOR CONSTRUCTION

This combination text and workbook shows and tells how to read residential, commercial, and light industrial prints. With an abundance of actual drawings from the construction industry, you learn step-by-step about each component of a set of blueprints, even cost estimating. 336 pp.; Goodheart - Willcox (spiral bound)

$26.00

Book No. 2628
THE VISUAL HANDBOOK OF BUILDING & REMODELING

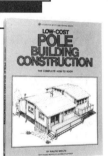

This book addresses many common questions about what materials to specify for your new home. It focuses on explaining technical information relating to various materials, which are important to the construction of a quality home. Illustrations and organized lists make this the ideal materials reference source for the do-it-yourselfer. 498 pp.; Rodale Press (hardcover)

$39.95

Book No. 2626
LOW-COST POLE BUILDING CONSTRUCTION

This how-to book successfully attacks this unique type of construction. It is the "nuts and bolts" of how to actually build all kinds of pole building including sheds, barns and homes, at great savings over traditional construction techniques. There are detailed diagrams to help in the entire project including heating, plumbing, and electrical. 182 pp.; Garden Way (paperback)

$12.95

Book No. 2634
MODERN RESIDENTIAL WIRING

Everything a person needs to know about wiring their home is explained in detail with an abundance of diagrams. Specifics from what tools are needed, to electrical trouble shooting are included, as well as safety grounding essentials, appliance wiring, and much more. 272 pp.; Goodheart-Willcox (hardcover)

$23.80

Book No. 2518
BUILD YOUR OWN HOME

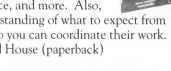

This is an authoritative guide on how to be your own general contractor. It goes through the step-by-step process of building a house with emphasis in the business aspects such as financing, scheduling, permits, insurance, and more. Also, it gives an understanding of what to expect from subcontractors so you can coordinate their work. 112 pp.; Holland House (paperback)

$12.95

Book No. 2596
HOW TO GET IT BUILT

No matter how small or how large your construction project is, building will be easier with this informative guidebook. Guidelines have been carefully prepared to follow step-by-step cost saving construction methods. Written by an architect/contractor, this book offers home owners cost saving solutions to his own building needs. 238 pp.; over 300 illus.; Hashagen (paperback)

$22.00

Book No. 2632
HOW TO BE YOUR OWN ARCHITECT

The book for people who know what they want in their home and want to design it themselves. Typical problems and solutions are presented in a very understandable way, with every step in the home design process included. Even site selection and financing are addressed. 235 pp.; over 200 illus.; Betterway Publications (paperback)

$18.95

Book No. 2605
CONTRACTING YOUR HOME

With over 150 illustrations, this guide offers many suggestions and ideas on contracting your home. Many forms that can be copied and reused are provided, giving checklists and glossary of terms used by the professionals, as well as all the necessary estimating forms. 279 pp.; Betterway Publications (paperback)

$18.95

Book No. 2570
MODERN MASONRY

Everything you will ever need to know about concrete, masonry, and brick is included in this book. Forms construction, concrete reinforcement, proper foundation construction, and bricklaying are among the topics covered in step-by-step detail. An excellent all-round reference and guide. 256 pp.; 700 illus.; Goodheard - Willcox (hardcover)

$23.80

BOOK No. 2504
ARCHITECTURE, RESIDENTIAL, DRAWING & DESIGN

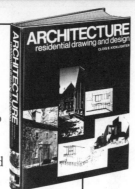

An excellent text that explains all of the fundamentals on how to create a complete set of construction drawings. Specific areas covered include proper design and planning considerations, foundation plans, floor plans, elevations, stairway details, electrical plans, plumbing plans, and more. 492 pp.; over 800 illus.; Goodheart - Willcox (hardcover)

$33.00

BOOK No. 2516
BUILDING CONSULTANT

The new home buyer's bible to home construction. This encyclopedia of home building explains in comprehensive detail all about the various elements that go into a completed house. It enables you to deal with the construction of your new home in a way that will avoid costly errors, whether you use a contractor or build it yourself. 188 pp.; Holland House (paperback)

$12.95

BUILD-IT-YOURSELF BOOKS ORDER INFORMATION

FOR FASTEST SERVICE CALL OUR TOLL-FREE NUMBER AND CHARGE-IT! 1-800-235-5700

All foreign residents call 1-203-632-0500
Or FAX your Credit Card order to 203-632-0712

Send your check, money order or credit card information to:

THE GARLINGHOUSE COMPANY, 34 Industrial Park Place, P.O. Box 1717, Middletown, CT 06457
No C.O.D. orders accepted; U.S. funds only.
UPS will not ship to Post Office Boxes, APO Boxes, Alaska or Hawaii
Prices subject to change without notice.

SHIPPING CHARGES	FIRST BOOK	EACH ADD'L BOOK
UPS (7 - 10 Working Days)	$5.00	$0.50
1st Class (APO, FPO, P.O. Boxes, AK, HI)	$6.50	$0.50
CANADA (Air Parcel Post)	$6.50	$1.50

BUILD-IT-YOURSELF BOOKS ORDER FORM

Order Code No.: **B3SM5**

YES! PLEASE SEND ME THE FOLLOWING BOOKS:

QUANTITY	BOOK NO. & TITLE	PRICE
_____	_____	$ _____
_____	_____	$ _____
_____	_____	$ _____
_____	_____	$ _____

CREDIT CARD INFORMATION
Charge To: ☐ Visa ☐ Mastercard ☐ Discover
Card # |_|_|_|_|_|_|_|_|_|_|_|_|_|_|_|_|_|_|_|
Signature _____ Exp. ___/___

SHIPPING CHARGES: First Book $ _____
Add'l Books $ _____
RESIDENT SALES TAX: $ _____
(KS - 5.9%, CT - 6%)
TOTAL ENCLOSED $ _____

BILL TO: (address must be as it appears on credit card statement)

Name_____ (Please Print)   Daytime Phone (_____) _____

Address_____ City/State _____ Zip _____

SHIP TO: (if different from Bill To):

Name_____

Address_____ City/State _____ Zip _____
(UPS will not ship to P.O. Boxes)